A SOURCE OF PRIDE

Regimental Badges and Titles
in the Canadian Expeditionary Force 1914–1919

Joseph H Harper

D1501154

Service Publications
PO Box 33071
Ottawa, Ontario K2C 3Y9

This edition first published in Canada,
July, 1999 by
Service Publications,
P.O. Box 33071
Ottawa, Ontario K2C 3Y9
Ph - 613-820-7350
Fax - 613-820-1288
service@magi.com

ISBN 0-9699845-8-8

Printed and bound in Canada
Cover design by Clive M. Law

Canadian Cataloguing in Publication Data

Harper, Joseph, H., 1927 — A source of pride: badges of the
Canadian Expeditionary Force, 1914–1919

Includes bibliographical references.
ISBN 0-9699845-8-8

1. Canada. Canadian Army. Canadian Expeditionary Force —
Medals, badges, decorations, etc. I. Title

UC535.C3H37 1999   355.1'342   C99-900690-8

Cover photo, Cap badge and collar badges of
the Yukon Motor Machine Gun Battery, worn
here by Capt Meurling, MC.
National Archives of Canada, PA2535

Table of Contents

Introduction

*. . . our Canadian Troops in the CEF . . . have the same
feeling of pride in their own badges, and what they stand for,
as has been so outstanding for years in the British Army*

Brig-Gen H D B Ketchen, CMG
Commanding 6th Canadian Infantry
Brigade

Collectors have been fascinated with CEF badges for many years. There were many units with distinctive badges – over 260 infantry units alone. When we look deeper, we find that some of the badges were approved officially by Headquarters in Ottawa, London or France; some were introduced by the unit's Officer Commanding and further approval was not requested or received; some were provided by makers without approval; some were make-shift (interim) issues; and some were prototypes or experimental designs. There are even a few that may not be genuine! This paper will describe the use of badges in the CEF, how they were introduced and the approvals that were given, sometimes long after the fact.

Early in the war, badges were obtained by units raised in Canada on the authority of the officer commanding the unit, brigade or division. In some instances the badges of the permanent force or militia regiments or corps were used. By May 1915, a process was being followed in some cases where the Minister of Militia in Ottawa approved badge designs. The Author has not been able to find any formal documentation of this process and communication of it throughout the CEF. Consequently the process was followed by only some of the units. Some units believed that since the badges were paid for by the unit from non-public regimental funds, militia headquarters approval was not necessary. Some units applied for approval after the badges were issued. In some cases the unit continued to wear its badges even after the design was rejected. In some cases a badge design was rejected solely because the word "Overseas" did not appear on the badge. The unit then had the badge made with "Overseas" on it obviously assuming that approval was implied. Also, there did not appear to be any documented process to obtain approval from Headquarters Overseas Military Forces of Canada (OMFC), London of the badge designs for those units formed overseas. Information on badges in their files and Canadian Corps Headquarters files are incomplete. At the end of January 1917 the Canadian Corps Headquarters Building was destroyed by fire and all records were lost. It appears that most badges were either approved by the branch directors at headquarters OMFC or the Corps commanders in France. It was not until October 1917 that a policy to use public funds was established to supply all the units in the field with their badges from the Canadian Ordnance Depot.

Official sources consulted were the files on badges found in the OMFC/CEF records and the Department of Militia and Defence records held by the National Archives of Canada in Ottawa. The badge files of individual CEF units and all but two of the Military Districts in Canada have not survived.

The Historical Section, Canadian War Records Office in London began to assemble a collection of regimental badges and devices used in the CEF in the summer of 1917 (A copy of the Section's Report on the collection is reproduced in Appendix 16.) They wrote each unit requesting specimens of their cap and collar badges and shoulder titles. The records kept while this collection was being assembled are also in the National Archives. These were consulted as well. The collection is found in the Canadian War Museum today. Also consulted were pictures and notes in the Author's possession of some of the deceased "first generation" badge collectors. They started collecting during World War I or shortly thereafter so their information on badges was first-hand.

Throughout this paper references are made to the illustrations of badges found in W K Cross' books or Babin's booklet on CEF badges. The illustrations of badges in this paper are those not found in either. One can only assume parts of the story on the evolution badges in the CEF. Where I have used words such as "probably", "likely", "assume", it indicates I have made a considered assumption. Anyone having photographic or other evidence that either supports or disproves these assumptions is encouraged to forward such information to the writer.

Many people contributed to this project. My thanks to the staff of the reading room of the National Archives of Canada, to Major Paul Lansey, Heritage Officer, Directorate of History and Heritage at National Defence Headquarters, to Helen Holt, Conservator, Dress & Insignia, Canadian War Museum, to Barry Agnew, Military Curator, Glenbow Museum to Lindsay Moir, Senior Librarian and the staff of the Glenbow Library and Archives, to Maurice Doll, Curator Government History, Provincial Museum of Alberta., and to Bruce Ibsen, City Archivist and the staff of the City of Edmonton Archives. Sgt Greg Gallant, Curator, Prince Edward Island Regiment Military Museum provided me with information on the badges of PEI units. Ron Edwards of Powell River, B C generously provided me with the results of his research into Canadian Machine Gun Corps badges. Bob Russell of Victoria loaned me some of the rare and unusual badges in his collection. Victor Taboika, Elbow Military Museum, Calgary gave me access to his extensive collection of uniforms and photographs. Wayne Cline loaned me documents and pictures of the Will R Bird collection. LCol Wyn van der Schee (ret'd), Calgary helped me in many ways. The Curators of several Regimental Museum also provided me with useful information. My thanks also to Clive Law of Service Publications for publishing this paper and to Charles (Chuck) Hamilton for providing photographs of CEF soldiers from his private collection.

I owe a special debt of gratitude to some of the "first generation" badge collectors, Sam Bailey, Will R. Bird, Bill Bone, Major W K Clawson, Dick Cox, Robert Duncan, Capt Philippe Durand and Charles B Hill-Tout. Some of them served in the CEF and began collecting overseas. They are no longer with us, but with their strong interest in CEF badges, they did more than simply collect pieces of metal. They studied and gathered information about their badges and fortunately left notes and photographs which have been of tremendous help in this project. Some of these gentlemen I knew through correspondence, others I met in person and we talked at length about badges. My collecting of Canadian badges spans 58 years and during that time I have made extensive notes of information obtained on CEF badges.

I also want to say thanks to my son Grant for reviewing the draft and to my daughter-in-law, Laureen, of Page Creations, for her professional advice and preparation of the illustrations and text for publishing.

Joe Harper
Calgary, Alberta
May, 1999

Chapter 1

Policies and Practices For Badges

The Outbreak of War

When war was declared Canada's military comprised a small permanent force and a fairly large active militia. Badges for these units were authorized in general orders. The permanent force were provided with badges and titles through Ordnance Stores. The cap badges for the active militia were acquired from regimental funds, but collar badges and shoulder numerals were available through Ordnance Stores. In August 1914 the permanent force and active militia units were placed on active service. The militia units were called upon to provide volunteers to the 1st Canadian Contingent CEF mobilizing at Valcartier, Quebec.

The General Service Maple Leaf Badge

The Canadian units serving in the South African War 1899 – 1901 were the first to wear a General Service maple leaf badge on their head-dress. It was a large badge, 2 ¼" high and 2" wide, with the Queen Victoria crown over a CANADA scroll on the maple leaf.[1] There was a smaller collar badge of the same design. On 1 February 1912 the Staff Orderly Service, Section "B" Corps of Military Staff Clerks was formed. Their badges were approved that year and were the same design as the former 1899 – 1901 General Service maple leaf badges but smaller and with the Tudor (King's) crown. The cap badge was in gilding metal and the collar badges in bronze. These were the badges, usually in bronze, that were adopted as the general service badges for the CEF (figure 1). They were provided to units at public expense through Ordnance Stores.[2]

Type A   Type B   Type C

Type D   Type E

Figure 1 *Five types of General Service Maple Leaf cap badges (reduced size)*

Author's Collection

Official Approval of Badges

Prior to the war, official approval of distinctive badges for Canadian Militia regiments and corps was published in General Orders issued by militia headquarters. However, for CEF units in Canada requesting official approval of a distinctive design badge by the Minister of Militia, such approval was given to the unit by letter from the Secretary, Militia Council or the Quartermaster General Canadian Militia to the District Officer Commanding the Divisional Area or Military District in which the CEF unit was being raised. A General Order was not issued for approval of CEF unit badges.

When the CEF units arrived in the UK the situation was not as straight forward. Approval was given for distinctive badges for units overseas by various Headquarters or Commands as follows:

- GOC 1st Canadian Contingent. Verbal approval was given by the GOC to Battalions of the 1st Contingent to introduce distinctive badges.
- HQ Canadian Training Division (CTD). Approval was given for distinctive badges to at least the 30th and 32nd Battalions by HQ CTD.
- HQ Overseas Military Forces of Canada (OMFC) in London by Chief of Staff or Branch Directors.
- Canadian Corps HQ. Approval was likely given by the Corps Commander. The HQ building was destroyed by fire at the end of January 1917 and many files were destroyed.

The 1st Canadian Contingent CEF

The permanent force units placed on active service in the CEF wore their approved badges. The contingents provided by the militia comprised volunteers from their respective units plus additional men recruited for service. When these volunteer contingents arrived at Valcartier camp outside of Quebec city in 1914 they were either wearing their militia regimental badges, were issued the General Service maple leaf badges. or were without any badges.[3] These contingents were formed into sixteen infantry battalions, and a number of artillery and other units during September 1914. The 17th Battalion was not formed until 22 September. The 1st Contingent sailed for the United Kingdom on 3 October.

Figure 2 A member of the 101st Regiment (Edmonton Fusiliers) Overseas Contingent August 1914 before leaving for Valcartier. The arm band reads (in part) "101" "Overseas".

NAC PA 200684

Distinctive Badges for Units of the 1st Contingent

With the haste in organizing the 1st Contingent it is doubtful that anything was done about distinctive badges for the newly created units. While the 9th Battalion was at Valcartier they received authority from the Minister of Militia for the Officers to continue to wear the 101st Edmonton Fusiliers badges.[4] Distinctive badges were acquired by the battalions and other units after arriving in the UK. Few files on badges for the 1st Contingent units are extant so it is not known precisely when the badges were designed or introduced. It is known that the Officer Commanding (OC) 2nd Infantry Brigade submitted designs for the cap badges for the 5th, 6th, 7th and 8th Battalions to the AAG i/c Administration for approval on 26 October 1914. He also stated in the letter "All battalions desire to wear the maple leaf as the collar badge"[5]. In a further letter dated 10 November 1914 to Canadian Contingent Headquarters he advised that:

Figure 3 10th Battalion makeshift cap badge
Bob Russell collection

> . . . in accordance with verbal instructions from General Alderson, this date, the Regimental devices submitted with the above quoted letter will be adopted.[5]

The OC 12th Reserve Battalion wrote a year later that General Alderson, GOC 1st Canadian Contingent announced at a meeting of Officers during October/November 1914 "that there must be distinctive badges for each unit", A representative of Hicks & Sons came down to Salisbury Plain to take orders.[6] Hicks & Sons account for the 12th Battalion cap badges and cloth shoulder flashes had been forwarded for audit on 25 January 1915.[7] On 26 November 1914 the Colonel Commanding West Down South, Shorncliffe stated that badges were being made for the 13th, 14th and 15th Battalions.[8] Only the badges of the 14th Battalion were approved by militia headquarters in Ottawa and this did not occur until 15 October 1915. Collar badges consisting of a C over numeral were introduced in the late fall 1914 and made by Elkington & Company.[9] These were made for all seventeen battalions of the 1st Contingent.

Make-shift cap badges comprising "1" or "2" on the General Service maple leaf were found in two of the "older" badge collections. These probably were worn – see "Makeshift Battalion Badges", Chapter 8. Distinctive badges for the 10th Battalion were not introduced until mid 1916.[10] Two types of makeshift maple leaf cap badges are known to exist for the 10th Battalion. One was an Officers' badge (Cross 10B) which is in the collection of the Provincial Museum

Figure 4 Early Officer's badge of the 10th Battalion
Provincial Museum of Alberta

of Alberta. It definitely was worn (figure 4). The other badge may have been an Other Ranks makeshift cap badge (figure 3).[11]

Dress Regulations for the 1st Division were published in 1st Division Routine Order (RO) 1378, 8 November 1915 covering badges:

It is noticed that there is a great diversity in Dress in the various infantry units of this Division. The GOC desires the following instructions strictly observed:-

Officers will wear on the cap and on the collar of the service jacket the Maple Leaf, or, in the case of Battalions which have adopted a regimental badge common to the whole battalion, the Regimental Crest of their unit.

On the shoulder strap of the service jacket the badge Canada only will be worn.

Regimental Officers and other Officers below the rank of Colonel are not to wear rank badges on the shoulder straps.

Warrant Officers, NCO's and Men will wear on the cap Maple Leaf, or, in the case of battalions who have adopted a regimental badge common to the whole battalion, the Regimental Crest of their unit.

On the collar they will wear the badge $\frac{C}{1} : \frac{C}{2}$ and nothing else.

On the shoulder strap the badge Canada only will be worn.

Units should apply to Divisional Headquarters through the usual channel for any badge required.

Badges for Further CEF Units

After the 1st Contingent left Canada for overseas, the 2nd Division CEF and many reinforcing units were authorized. Usually, General Service maple leaf badges were worn by the units before the introduction of its distinctive design badges. After arrival in the UK, C over numeral collar badges were made for the battalions of the 2nd Division and the 23rd, 30th, 32nd, 33rd reserve battalions. There are a number of makeshift (interim) badges[12] in existence with the battalion number on the General Service maple leaf. These may have been worn by the battalion before it received its distinctive badges. It is known that the 49th Battalion Officers wore the numerals 49 below the General Service maple leaf badge on the cap[13] (figure 5) before they obtained the first issue of their battalion pattern badges.

In both Canada and the UK the OC of a unit was permitted to introduce distinctive badges provided this was at regimental expense. It was not until May 1915 than any of

Figure 5 *Lieutenant George Z Pinder, 49th Battalion showing the makeshift cap badge*

NAC PA 185339

these badges introduced in Canada were approved by the Minister of Militia. However, the approval procedure was not always followed. Militia District (MD) No 2 scrupulously followed the approval process. It was outlined in two letters during September 1915 and February 1916.[14] Some of the MD No 2 units did not ask for approval of their badges, and in those cases follow-up letters were sent to the OC. On the other hand, only three of the units raised in MD No 11 had their badges approved. To illustrate, here is a summary of the badge approvals for the 1st to 13th Regiments Canadian Mounted Rifles and the 18th to 258th Battalions raised after the 1st Contingent left Canada:

Figure 6 A soldier wearing the cap and collar badges of the 90th Battalion

Charles Hamilton collection

| | Number of Units | |
| | Badges | Badges Not |
Units Raised In	**Approved**	**Approved**
1st Divisional Area/MD No 1 (Western Ontario)	7	12
2nd Divisional Area/MD No 2 (Central Ontario)	45	12
3rd Divisional Area/MD No 3 (Eastern Ontario)	14	9
4th & 5th Divisional Areas/MD Nos 4 & 5 (Quebec)	11	12
6th Divisional Area/MD No 6 (Maritimes)	10	12
MD No 10 (Manitoba & Saskatchewan)	35	19
MD No 11 (British Columbia & Yukon)	3	17
MD No 13 (Alberta)	12	10
Several MDs	11	3
	148	106

Controversy about the Badges worn Overseas

It was not until 1916 that the question of approved badges was taken seriously by the authorities in London. On 17 February 1916 the Chief Ordnance Officer (COO) of the CEF at the Canadian Ordnance Depot, Ashford, Kent wrote Major-General J W Carson, Canadian General Staff, deploring the situation:

Figure 7 *Unapproved Officers' cap badges of the 30th, 47th and 48th Battalions*

Author's collection

I may say that there is a general tendency on the part of Commanding Officers, to want to introduce special pattern badges of their own design, and at the present time, I know there are several of these fancy badges in existence. A representative of a Birmingham manufacturer was here the other day, with samples of badges, and several that he had were not recognized. Enquiry elicited the fact that the firm had been asked to prepare new designs. Several were made, and the unit I suppose, selected what they liked best, or that which was considered the prettiest.

As regards the "C" numerals, I understand that in some battalions, the Commanding Officers ordered the removal of the maple leaf from the collars of the serge jackets, in order to substitute the numeral, under what authority this was done, I do not know, but the fact remains that we look to Canada for our supply of badges, and many thousands are sent over, and I can only assume, that any article we receive from Canada, must be accepted as the sealed or standard pattern, and not one of these numerals with the letter "C" have we received from there.

The whole question of these badges is one that might well be taken up, and a decision be arrived at regarding what should, or should not be worn by our troops.[16]

He further stated that:

. . . as far as this department is concerned the only official badges authorized to be worn by Canadian Infantry Battalions are the following:
In Forage or Service Cap – Large Maple Leaf
In collar of Serge Jacket – Small Maple Leaf

Regarding the C over numeral badges he mentioned that a large number were turned into the stores at Salisbury when the 1st Division went to the front and were subsequently issued by his staff to get rid of them. The COO stated that these "were evidently purchased regimentally by the Commanding Officer, whether on their own responsibility or not I am unable to say".

Figure 8 *Unapproved Officers' collar badge of the 7th Battalion[15]*

Author's collection

However the Director of Equipment and Ordnance Stores (DEOS) wrote the Commander-in-Chief of the BEF the next day:

> . . . that the representative of the Canadian Department of Militia and Defence in this country states that the letter "C" in addition to the numerals worn as collar badges by Canadian Units, has been authorized, and that as far as possible demands for numerals of this pattern will be met.[17]

This confirmed that C over numeral was worn as collar badges by units in France. Meanwhile in Ottawa, the QMG advised the Chief of the General Staff on 26 April 1916 that:

> The badges supplied to every Overseas Unit consists of –
>   Cap Badge – Large Maple Leaf with "Canada" on it.
>   Collar Badge – The same only smaller.
>   Shoulder Title – "Canada" in one word.
> But in very many cases Officers commanding have submitted Badges of special design. These are as a rule designed with a Maple Leaf background. And every effort is made to induce Officers to use this design. It is possible some units may be wearing badges that have not been approved.[18]

In another letter to The Secretary War Office dated 25 May 1916.[19] The Chief Ordnance Officer laid out his understanding of the official policy for badges in use by the CEF at the time:

> I have the honour to forward herewith samples of the following badges which are supplied from Canada for units of the Canadian Expeditionary Force:
>   (1) Badges, cap, Maple Leaf (large)
>   (2) Badges, collar, Maple Leaf (small)
> The following are details given in regard to the above mentioned badges:
> (1) & (2) According to information furnished by the Principal Ordnance Officer, Ottawa, these are the only cap and collar badges provided by the public for units of the Canadian Expeditionary Force, but it is stated that authority has been given for special badges for units who have applied for same, but at their own expense.

It is interesting to note that the above did not contain any reference to the C over numeral collar badges being supplied to the 1st Division.[20]

By May 1916 the Canadian Corps in the field consisted of Corps Troops and three Divisions. The 4th Division was still in training in England. There were thirty-six battalions in the field and the badges of only three battalions, the 14th, 25th and 60th, had received official approval from militia headquarters in Ottawa. However, half of the twelve infantry battalions of the 4th Divisions had their badges approved.

To clarify the proper wearing of badges by troops in the field Canadian Corps Routine Order 592 was issued on 20 May 1916 stating:

> It has been noticed that some Officers, NCO's and men have been wearing the badge of a unit other than that to which they belong.

The only occasion when Officers or men not serving with a unit are permitted to wear the badges of the unit is when they are seconded or attached for special duty, or employed on command, that is to say, not struck off the strength of their unit.

Also, badges were being sold in retail stores in London and Folkestone and neighbouring villages. The Assistant Provost Marshall at Bramshott Camp requested retail stores at the camp and neighbouring villages withdraw from the sale of badges. George F Hemsley Co. Limited objected but they were firmly advised that the restrictions on the sale of Canadian badges at Bramshott would stand. However, there was no objection to the sale of Officers' or enameled badges.[21]

Representations from the Field

The Corps Commander, Lieutenant-General Hon Sir Julian Byng had issued Canadian Corps Routine Order 678, 2 June 1916 stating:

> The Corp Commander, wishes that the question of badges throughout the CEF should be settled as early as possible. With this in view, all units that have not done so, will forward to Headquarters, Canadian Corps, through Divisions, a sample of the badge in use or suggested.

General Byng wrote Second Army on 3 July that he:

> . . . should be glad if the Canadian Government would authorize the issue at the public expense of badges now worn at the front by units comprising the Corps under my command . . . At present these special badges are permitted by Canadian authorities on the understanding that units provide them at their own expense, and this is being done . . . Samples of these badges have been collected and can be forwarded to Canada if sanction is given to my recommendation.[16]

Major-General Arthur W Currie, Commanding 1st Canadian Division wrote Canadian Corps Headquarters on 29 July:

> All the battalions now have regimental badges, which I think should be worn on the cap instead of the plain maple leaf. The order of Dress, so far as badges are concerned, I recommend is, therefore, as follows:
>
> | On the cap: | Regimental Badge | All ranks. |
> | On the collar: | Regimental Badge | Officers. |
> | | C/1; C/2 &c.&c. | Other Ranks[19] |

On 16 August General Byng forwarded to HQ Second Army a statement showing collar badges recommended together with specimens of the actual cap badges and shoulder titles in use by the three Divisions and Corps Troops in the field. These were the cap and shoulder badges worn by the units after mobilization. He also stated that:

. . . the collar badge, i.e. "C" with numeral is worn by a number of units at present, and General Officers Commanding Divisions are unanimous in recommending that this form of collar badge should be universal for Infantry Units. The GOC 3rd Canadian Division recommends that CMR Battalions wear the collar badge as shown on the statement, i.e. number with "CMR" underneath.[22]

Discussions at Headquarters

The recommendations of General Byng generated considerable discussion at CEF HQ in London and Militia HQ, Ottawa. The issue was brought before the Militia Council. On 12 December 1916 and 10 January 1917 the Council reached a decision on the badges to be worn by units serving in France.[23] One part of the decision was that all the infantry battalions were to wear only the General Service maple leaf as

Figure 9 Sgt F G Coppins, VC, 8th Battalion CEF

NAC PA-6765

their cap badge, C over numeral as the collar badges and only the CANADA shoulder title. The pioneer battalions were to wear the General Service maple leaf cap and collars. This meant that many of the units were to lose their distinctive cap badges and some their distinctive shoulder titles.

The new policy was outlined in Canadian Corps Routine Order 1041, 30 January 1917. It prompted negative reactions from some of the battalions:

> *The OC 42nd Battalion stated:* I feel very strongly that being deprived of our distinctive badge we would lose the traditions of the Home regiment and those of the famous regiment to which we have the honour to be affiliated. These are particularly valuable in helping to create a good regimental spirit.[24]
> *The OC 49th Battalion wrote:* I think that it is of greater importance that Battalion Commanders should be able to identify quickly their own men. In action, and in the case of dead and wounded men, where Canadians are engaged, the maple leaf cap badge is of little or no use as identification.[25]
> *The OC 72nd Battalion also noted:* the cap badge is the badge worn by our parent unit, the 72nd Regiment, Seaforth Highlanders of Canada, Vancouver, Canada. It is eminently suited to the balmoral or glengarry . . . I would like very much to have permission to continue wearing these badges . . .[26]

Brigadier-General Ketchen, Commanding 6th Canadian Infantry Brigade also wrote Headquarters 2nd Canadian Division on 9 February 1917 stating the case for distinctive badges very eloquently and at some length:

> It is submitted, that the conditions of this order mean the giving up by Battalions of distinctive badges, worn since organization – and which in most instances are practically, apart for names of Battalions, the only visible links between them and their territorial connections.

These badges were originally provided as gifts to Battalions at considerable expense by Provincial Governments and Cities in Canada on mobilization[27], and were approved by Militia Headquarters in Ottawa.

They have been worn by Battalions throughout the campaign – in the Salient and at the Somme – and have been a source of much pride to Officers and men, as being one of the few facts – organized, as our Canadian Battalions are, from particular localities in the Dominion – which have assisted in keeping up Esprit de Corps, and Battalion spirit, no matter what changes occurred in their make-up or personnel.

Most of these original badges were adopted to commemorate, not only home connections of Battalions, but with a view to perpetuating their origin from Militia Battalions, Brigades, and Military Districts in Canada, which conditions cannot be met by badges made up of the numerals of Battalions.

It is thought that the historical records of Battalions are of necessity meagre enough, raised as our Canadian Troops have been, and the withdrawal of distinctive badges, adopted on organization with the direct intention of assisting in keeping up Battalion associations, Battalion spirit, esprit de corps and pride of origin, removes the only existing link in this direction.

I feel certain, that notwithstanding the short existence so far of our Canadian Troops in the CEF, that they have the same feeling of pride in their own badges, and what they stand for to them, as has been so outstanding for years in the British Army.

One of the first things that our reinforcements do on arriving is to provide themselves with their Unit's badges, showing that there exists a strong and distinct feeling of pride in all ranks as regards their local and home traditions, and which it is suggested might well be up-held by the free issue of the original badges of Canadian Battalions, rather than abolishing them altogether.[28]

Fortunately the Militia Council reconsidered its decision on badges and on 2 February 1917 rescinded their decision.[23] No reasons appear in the Minutes. The QMG in Ottawa cabled the QMG CEF in the UK a week later of the decision to rescind.[29] This was communicated throughout the Canadian Corps by Corps RO 1092. At this point the whole question of badges fell into limbo.

Policy on Badges finally Established

Sir George Perley was appointed "Minister of Overseas Military Forces of Canada in the United Kingdom" on 31 October 1916. Sir George resurrected the idea of a new policy on badges for the CEF in the field. A memo to Sir Edward Kemp, Minister of Militia written 2 May 1917 stated in part:

My opinion, based upon that of the Corps Commander, at the Front, the Quartermaster General and the Director of Ordnance Service here, is that proper badges should be adopted and supplied to the units both in England and France at public expense. Many requests are being received from Officers Commanding units in both countries, as there is a distinct disciplinary side to the question. Failing the adoption and supply of badges of a stock pattern the men provide themselves with all sorts of fancy badges sold by civilians, with the result that the appearance of the men is by no means what it should be. Distinctive unit badges are supplied by Imperial authorities and I see no reason why the same practice should not be followed by us.[30]

Late in August each of the Divisions sent Canadian Corps Headquarters a statement[31] showing for each unit:

- Badges to be worn
- Source of supply; maker and present possessor of dies
- Price per gross
- Annual requirements

The Canadian Ordnance Depot in turn prepared a consolidated statement adding the units in the Corps Troops. Appendix 8 gives the Source of Supply of badges in use in the field at that time.

The Militia Council at their 1 June 1917 meeting recommended the purchase of badges for the units overseas.[23] As a result of Sir George's initiative an official policy on the wearing and supply of badges for the Canadian Corps was established finally. A memorandum was issued by Canadian Corps HQ to all Commands on 27 October 1917.[32] This made official the practice that had been followed for the most part by units in the field since 1915, except that now the badges would be provided from public funds. The collar badges provided to infantry battalions (except for the CMR battalions) were C over numeral. These were to be worn by the Other Ranks[33], but the Officers for the most part continued to wear the battalion pattern collar badges.[34]

Figure 10 *85th Battalion (Nova Scotia Highlanders) other ranks sporran bearing the battalion badge.*

The Army Museum, Halifax, N.S.

J W Tiptaft and Son, Birmingham were selected as the supplier of the badges to the Canadian Ordnance Depot. An order was placed on 6 March 1918[35] for the following sets (cap and pair of collar badges):

Canadian Light Horse (each squadron)	200
Canadian Engineers	1,000
Infantry (each battalion)	1,000

Canadian Machine Gun Corps	2,000
Canadian Corps Cyclist Battalion	500
Canadian Military Police Corps	500

A *List of Badges authorized by the GOC Canadian Corps to be worn by Canadian Units in France* was sent by the QMG to the Secretary War Office on 25 June 1918. Illustrations of the badges were not part of the list, the letter merely stating:

> . . . the majority of these Badges are available for issue from the Canadian Ordnance Depot at Ashford at the present time. The remainder are coming in daily from the Contractor and will be made available as early as possible.[36]

General Routine Order (GRO) 4663 effective 1 August 1918 gave the formal approval for the special badges worn by all Canadian Corps units. (A copy of GRO 4663 is reproduced in Appendix 9.) After the armistice the Ordnance Depot at Ashford took inventory of their badges. (A copy of the inventory is reproduced in Appendix 11.) This shows the badges that were being issued by the Canadian Ordnance Depot by the end of the war.

Post Script

Earlier in the chapter, the Author described the reaction that occured when the Militia Council tried to eliminate distinctive badges for individual battalions. An item appeared in the *Manitoba Free Press*, Winnipeg, 24 March 1919 as the troops were returning from overseas. It describes how a Private felt about the badge of his unit:

> The esprit de corps of the Canadians in the field, their love, respect and pride in their different units, is well exemplified by a short verse picked up on the battlefield of Arras on Sept. 1, 1918. The writer was Pte. C. W. Bannister, who was killed on that date. He had written the poem on the back of an envelope by the light of a candle while resting in his dug-out, preparatory to going over the top. Pte. Bannister was with the 5th battalion [and their] badge is backed by red flannel.

OUR BADGE

The crown, it stands for loyalty
    To empire, home, and king,
The Fifth will never waver
    in the faith to which they cling.

A prancing horse, a royal crown,
    A blood red band beneath
With Western cavalry engraved,
    Surrounded by a wreath

The wreath, it stands for glory
    And honors bravely won,
Foremost in war, foremost in work,
    Foremost in sport and fun.

The horse, it stands for nobleness,
    And gameness to the end,
Proven in many a conflict
    To be man's truest friend.

That little piece of cloth beneath,
    That band of crimson red,
It tells how free in Flanders,
    Canadian blood was shed.

Chapter 2

Reinforcing Unit Badges

Additional Battalions

After the 1st Contingent arrived on Salisbury Plain in the UK, twelve of the seventeen infantry battalions became part of the newly formed 1st Division. Of the other five battalions, the 6th was absorbed by the Remount Depot and the Canadian Cavalry Depot and the 9th, 11th, 12th and 17th were redesignated "Reserve Battalions". In November 1914, the 2nd Division was authorized to be formed in Canada. Shortly afterwards additional reinforcing battalions (33rd to 56th Battalions) were authorized. The 23rd, 30th, 32nd, 33rd and other Battalions also became "Reserve Battalions". During 1915–16 many more battalions (57th to 245th Battalions) were authorized. Recruiting began for the 246th to 255th Battalions in late 1916.

As the casualties in the trenches mounted there was an urgent need for reinforcements. But many of the newly authorized battalions were still training in Canada. These battalions were considered to be "draft-giving depot battalions" and they were asked to send reinforcing drafts immediately. They were usually of company or half-company size. Upon arrival in the UK they were absorbed by one of the reserve battalions. One of these, the 1st Reinforcing Draft from the 92nd Battalion (5 Officers and 250 Other Ranks) had a distinctive badge[c1] which was a kilt pin. It is not clear if this was ever worn on parade.[1] There is no record of authorization. During September 1915 it was decided to send whole battalions for reinforcements rather than drafts.[2]

Figure 11 Sgt Thomas Bradley, 147th Battalion

Author's collection

On 15 June 1915 The 79th Cameron Highlanders of Canada Overseas Drafting Detachment was formed to provide reinforcements to the 43rd Battalion. Four drafts were sent overseas during the last half of 1915. They used the glengarry badge of the parent militia regiment, but had a distinctive collar badge[3] (figure 12) There is no record of authorization for this collar badge. Another collar badge is known that also may have been used by the drafting detachment or the drafts sent overseas. It is of the 79th Cameron Highlanders of Canada[4] but the tablet at the base reads "BATTN C.E.F." "WINNIPEG" in two lines (figure 12).

Of the battalions raised during 1915–16, some were allotted to the 3rd, 4th or 5th Division after arrival in the UK. But most were used as reserve battalions. Even the infantry battalions of the 5th Division in the UK eventually were used as reinforcements.

Independent Companies/Drafts

During 1915–17 a number of independent companies or drafts were raised in Canada. On arrival overseas they were absorbed by one of the reserve battalions.

Distinctive badges for the Toronto University Infantry Company[c2] and No 1 Jewish Infantry Company[c3] were approved 16 May 1916 and 25 January 1917, respectively. No 1 Independent Infantry Company, Winnipeg, were granted permission on 10 February 1917 to wear the cap badge of the 27th Battalion. Badge specimens of the Yukon Infantry Company[c4] were sent to militia head-quarters 4 October 1917[5], but there is no record of approval on file. There also was a distinctive badge for the

Figure 12 Cameron Highlanders of Canada collar badges: Left – Overseas Drafting Detachment; Right – BATTN C.E.F inscription

Author's and Bob Russell collections

Overseas University Companies[c5] mobilized at McGill University to reinforce the Princess Patricia's Canadian Light Infantry. There is no record of approval of this badge. It is likely the General Service maple leaf badges were worn by any other independent companies or drafts.[6]

Drafts from Militia Units

In spite of intensive recruiting efforts most numbered battalions in Canada were not able to meet their full strength after mid 1916. Some battalions sailed overseas with a strength equivalent to three full companies and a few with only one or two companies. In January 1917 it was decided that raising new battalions would cease. Militia regiments were asked to recruit overseas drafts or companies (250 all ranks) for the CEF.[7] Forty-one militia regiments were authorized to raise overseas drafts. Special badges were struck for the 6th Regiment (Duke of Connaught's Own Rifles) Overseas Draft[c6], 11th Regiment (Irish Fusiliers of Canada) Overseas Draft[c7] and the 50th Regiment Overseas Draft[c8], all in MD No 11. These badges were introduced without authority. It is likely that some other of the overseas companies wore the badges of their parent militia regiment when they were in training in Canada. But when proceeding overseas General Service maple leaf badges would have been worn.[8]

The Territorial System

During January 1917 new organizations were put in place for the provision of reinforcements to units at the front and at the same time to provide a local territorial association between Canada and the units at the front. Twenty-six new reserve battalions were formed in the UK. Also, Territorial Regiments were created during March 1917. Each Territorial Regiment (which was an administrative unit) comprised the following:[9]

- One or more Depot Battalions in the particular MD in Canada.
- Regimental Depot in the UK.
- One or more Reserve Battalions in the UK.
- Each Reserve Battalion linked to two or more Battalions at the front or with the 5th Division in training in the UK. (The 5th Division infantry battalions were broken up in 1918 for reinforcements.)

Depot Battalions in Canada

Draft giving depot battalions were authorized in the MDs in Canada during 1917–18. Most of the recruits in training at the time of formation were absorbed and afterwards all new recruits and conscripts were posted to the Depot Battalion. Several of the Depot Battalions applied for permission to wear special badges, and this was denied.[10] The maple leaf cap and collar badges and a special shoulder title were approved for wear.[11] Soldiers of a Depot Battalion who had served overseas were permitted to wear the cap and collar badges of the unit with which they served overseas.[12] The 1st Depot Battalion Alberta Regiment had a crest approved which was used as the basis for their badges.[13, c9] Cap and collar badges were also introduced in the 1st and 2nd Depot Battalions British Columbia Regiment[c10], 1st and 2nd Depot Battalions 2nd Quebec Regiment[c11] and the 1st Depot Battalion Nova Scotia Regiment[c12] and a collar badge in the 1st Depot Battalion Manitoba Regiment (figure 13)[14], all without militia headquarters approval. Sweetheart pins are also known to have been made for some of the Depot Battalions that did not have special badges.[15]

Figure 13 1st Depot Bn Manitoba Regt collar badge[3]. (reduced)

Territorial Reserve Battalions in the United Kingdom

The territorial system resulted in the formation of some twenty-six new reserve battalions during January 1917. These were formed by amalgamating the former reserve battalions and infantry battalions available for reinforcements. The OC Canadian Training Division wrote Headquarters OMFC on 3 March 1917 proposing:

> A uniform cap and collar badge for all Reserve units is recommended, upon which may be superimposed the number of the Units. Shoulder numerals in plain brass, with the number and the letter "R", would not be expensive and would serve every purpose.
>
> On the receipt of a draft from Canada, the new badge and numerals would be issued. On a draft being ordered to proceed to France, the Reserve Battalion badges would be withdrawn for reissue, and any shortages paid for, and either the ordinary "Maple Leaf" badge with "Canada" shoulder badge and without numerals issued – or, a supply of special badge of the Unit in France to which the draft is proceeding, would be issued in exchange for the Reserve Unit badges.[16]

The proposal was abruptly dismissed nine days later:

> . . . on instructions received from the Department of Militia and Defence, Ottawa, it has been decided that no action is to be taken in the matter of having a uniform badge for Reserve Battalions.[17]

The 8th, 10th, 14th and 23rd Reserve Battalions went ahead and introduced distinctive badges anyway.[c13] The 14th Reserve Battalion even went so far as to submit the invoice for their cap badges to the Ordnance Depot for payment.[18] Tiptafts were encouraging the Reserve Battalions to order special badges. They wrote the 10th Reserve Battalion on 19 May 1917:

Figure 14 *4th Reserve Battalion cap badge*
Bob Russell collection

Figure 15 *12th Reserve cap badge*
Author's collection

. . . if you should be desiring badges, we beg to inform you that we have already executed orders for some of the Reserve Battalions, and we have, at the moment, an order in hand for another battalion. As far as our information goes from the battalions for whom we have executed orders, the decision rests with the Officer Commanding.[19]

Tiptafts also supplied the 8th and 23rd Reserve Battalions with their badges.[20]

The writer possesses an unusual badge of the 12th Reserve Battalion. It is in gilt with red and blue and enamel similar to a sweetheart pin but is cap size and has its original lugs, not a pin fastener (figure 15). It was likely custom made for a member of the 12th Reserve Battalion permanent staff. There is no makers name on the badge, but it appears to be a Tiptaft make. A similar design badge exists in brass with red enamel in centre for the 4th Reserve Battalion (figure 14).

During 1916–17 the Reserve Battalions were asked to submit samples of their badges to the Historical Section, Canadian War Records Office in London. Only a few responded. The 2nd, 7th, 18th and 25th Reserve Battalions stated they did not have special badges.[21] The 11th Reserve Battalion submitted badges which presumably were those of the original 11th Battalion.[22, c14] The 9th Reserve Battalion responded, ". . . this Battalion had no recognized badge either for Officers or Other Ranks."[23] It would seem that the well-known 9th Battalion badge[c15] was custom-made for individuals and not in general use in the Battalion.[24] The 8th Reserve Battalion submitted their special badge[25] which had not been approved.

It is quite likely that even when Reserve Battalions had special badges they were used only by the permanent staff of the Battalion, and that most of the Officers and men going through the battalion likely wore the badge of the unit they sailed with from Canada. Metal and enamel sweetheart pins are know to exist for a few of the Reserve Battalions.[26]

References – Cross' catalogue numbers

c1. 92D	c6. 266	c11. 25-11-1A	c13. 269
c2. 264	c7. 267	25-11-1B	270
c3. 261	c8. 268	25-11-2A	271
c4. 262	c9. 25-1-1	25-11-2B	272
c5. 265	c10.25-2-1	c12. 25-5-1	c14. 11
	25-2-2		c15. 9A

Chapter 3

Artillery Badges

Royal Canadian Horse Artillery

The Royal Canadian Horse Artillery Brigade was a unit of the permanent force at the outbreak of the war. It was mobilized for active service with the 1st Canadian Contingent. They wore a different badge from other artillery units[c1]. The badge had been approved in 1905 and was issued from Ordnance Stores. It was approved belatedly for the CEF on 1 August 1918 along with grenade collar badges. However, in June 1917 they were wearing the general issue Canada artillery gun cap badge.[1]

General Issue Artillery Badges

When war was declared in August 1914 the badges for the Canadian Artillery of the militia were:

> Forage cap: The gun with the scroll inscribed CANADA surmounted by the Crown; below the gun a scroll inscribed QUO FAS ET GLORIA DUCUNT.[c2]
>
> Service Dress cap: Grenade with scroll below inscribed CANADA.
>
> Collar: Grenade with scroll below inscribed CANADA.

The forage cap badge was adopted in the CEF as the general issue cap badge for artillery units. Its use in the CEF was approved formally in April 1918[2]. Collar badges used were either the General Service maple leaf badges or plain grenades. Unapproved versions of the Canada gun design cap badge exist with a wreath of maple leaves on either side of the gun[c3] as was a maple leaf badge with the gun design and "Overseas" on a tablet below the gun.[c4] One version of the gun badge with a wreath of maple leaves also had "Overseas Field Battery" on the rim of the gun wheel.[3]

Field Artillery

The 1st to 9th Batteries CFA were mobilized at Valcartier in September 1914 for the 1st Canadian Contingent. Probably some of the volunteers wore the artillery badges in use by the militia at the time and others the General Service maple leaf badges. The 10th, 11th and 12th Batteries were formed after the 1st Contingent arrived in the UK. The 13th to 28th

Figure 16 A gunner wearing the general issue Canada type artillery badge and General Service maple leaf collar badges

Charles Hamilton collection

Batteries were authorized for active service in the 2nd Division as of 7 November 1914.

Formation of the 29th to 43rd Batteries were authorized during 1915. The 36th Overseas Battery had distinctive badges,[c5] which were not approved. It is likely that the other batteries used either the General Service maple leaf badges issued by Ordnance Stores or the Canada gun badge purchased from battery funds.[4] MD No 2 took the position that the correct badges for CFA CEF units in Canada were "Cap badge – artillery badge; collar badges – maple leaf badges".[5]

The 44th to 78th Overseas Depot Batteries were authorized in 1916 and the 79th Overseas Depot Battery and 80th to 84th Overseas Batteries in 1917. Distinctive cap badges were approved for the 56th and 58th Depot Batteries.[c6,c7] The 58th Depot Battery had approved collar badges[c7] but distinctive collar badges for the 50th[c8] and the 63rd[c9] were not approved. The 46th and 64th Depot Batteries also had a distinctive badge[c10], and the 79th wore a grenade type badge for the winter fur cap[c11], all unapproved. Makeshift cap badges of the 8th, 15th 36th and 72nd Batteries CFA are known.[6] The Canadian War Museum collection has an unusual badge of the 40th Battery CFA.[7]

George F Hemsley Co Limited, of Montreal and at least one other Canadian maker produced cap badges for the 36th, 50th to 53rd, 55th to 57th, 61st to 79th Depot Batteries.[8] These were the Canada type artillery gun badge with or without a maple wreath. A separate wheel was mounted on the gun bearing the battery number in the centre and the wording "Overseas Field Battery" on the rim. The one exception was the separate wheel piece for the 67th Depot Battery. It bore the crest of the University of Toronto with the numeral "67" thereon and the wording "University of Toronto Overseas Battery" on the rim.[c12] Only the 79th Depot Battery badge[c13] of this group was approved. The 65th Depot Battery requested approval of the same design and it was denied! Also, the 70th Depot Battery requested approval of the Director of Artillery (DA) and received the following reply:

> . . . the D of A states in effect as follows: There should be no alterations in the badges as now issued to CEF Artillery Units. Depot Batteries in Canada have no claim, as Batteries, to the word "Overseas" on their Cap Badge. Batteries in the Field do not use this term.[9]

A similar type of unapproved cap badge was made for the 13th Brigade Headquarters with "13" on the wheel and the wording "Brigade Headquarters Overseas" on the rim.[c14]

While the special badges were worn in Canada they were discontinued upon arrival in the UK. The QMG OMFC wrote the QMG in Canada on 9 May 1918:

> I am directed to draw your attention to the fact that Drafts for Artillery Units arriving in England come with all sorts of unauthorised cap and collar badges, which apparently are purchased by the Unit themselves. As these are not acceptable to the Artillery in England or in France, which would appear to be only a waste of money. The only badge used by the Overseas Artillery is the ordinary General Service Artillery Badge.[10]

CEF (Canada) RO 682, 17 June 1918 clarified the matter of distinctive battery badges:

Attention is directed to Routine Order No 492 which will be strictly enforced. The practice of certain artillery units, wearing badges, which embody the number of the Depot Battery concerned is unauthorized.

The *Statement of Badges of Canadian Units* prepared August 1917 showed the following in use by the Artillery in the field: Cap Badge "as for RFA but with CANADA instead of UBIQUE"; Collar badges – "small maple leaf badge" – all supplied by "Canadian Ordnance".[11] On 22 October 1917 the Director of Ordnance Services stated to the AG that the artillery "are wearing either the Artillery Badges used in Canada, or the Maple Leaf".[12] GRO 4663 effective 1 August 1918 approved

Figure 17 A gunner wearing one of the unapproved numbered battery cap badges

Charles Hamilton collection

the Field Batteries in France wearing "Cap badge, artillery badge (with CANADA); Collar badges, grenades".

In the last few years badges have appeared in auctions that are purported to be for "Training Batteries" in the CEF. Specimens of most of these badges are in the Canadian War Museum CEF collection. They are the general issue Canada artillery cap badge with the numerals 1 to 9 and the letters A to E, H and T mounted on the wheel.[13] The Author has not been able to verify with any certainty that these are CEF badges and draws the reader's attention to the section "Makeshift Artillery Badges" in Chapter 8.

Heavy Artillery

The 1st Heavy Battery was mobilized August 1914 for the 1st Contingent. 2nd Heavy Battery was placed on active service on 7 November 1914. Nos 1 and 2 Heavy Battery Depots were mobilized 20 April 1915. They later became Nos 1 and 2 Siege Batteries. Nos 3 to 8 Overseas Batteries Siege Artillery and No 9 Depot Battery Siege Artillery were formed during 1915 – 16. No 10 Depot Battery Siege Artillery was formed in 1917. Nos 11 and 12 Siege Batteries were formed in the UK as part of the Reserve Artillery Depot.

At the outbreak of the war 1st Heavy Battery would have worn the Canada gun cap badge. Their Depot became No 1 Battery Siege Artillery. Reinforcements to No 1 Siege Battery were advised February 1916 that they should use the General Service maple leaf cap badge rather than the artillery gun badge.[14] Six of the Siege Batteries wore distinctive cap badges. These were approved for No 3, No 6 (McGill) and No 10 (NS) Batteries Siege Artillery[c15], but not approved for No 4, No 5 (PEI) and No 9 (NB) Batteries Siege Artillery.[c16] For one issue of No 6 (McGill) Battery Siege Artillery, collar badges were in matched pairs. A later variation of No 3 Siege Battery badges[c17] were not approved A sweetheart pin is known for the 107th (Canadian) Siege Battery.[15]

The Cobourg Heavy Battery Depot and a number of Siege Artillery Drafts were formed in 1917. Unapproved cap badges were used by the Cobourg Heavy Battery

Depot[c18] and the Nova Scotia Siege Artillery Draft.[c19] The McGill Overseas Siege Artillery Draft was granted permission to wear the cap badge of No 6 Siege Battery (McGill). There also were unapproved badges for the No 5 (PEI) Siege Artillery Draft[c20] and King's County PEI Siege Artillery Draft [c21].

It is not clear whether the Siege Batteries without distinctive badges wore the General Service maple leaf badges, the Canada artillery gun cap badge with maple leaf or grenade collar badges, or the unapproved maple leaf artillery badges[c4]. It is known that the Officers of the 10th Siege Battery wore the Canada artillery gun cap badge.[16] The 11th Siege Battery also wore the Canada artillery gun cap badge and Officers the artillery grenade collar badges with

Figure 18 Collar badge King's County PEI Siege Artillery Draft (enlarged)

Greg Gallant collection

CANADA scroll and Other Ranks the General Service maple leaf collar badges.[17] In August 1917 the Siege Batteries in the field were reported to be wearing the Canada artillery gun cap badge and General Service maple leaf collar badges[11]. Under GRO 4663 of August 1918 the collar badges approved were the grenades, but in practice there always seemed to be exceptions.

Ammunition Columns

Each of the five divisions had Ammunition columns and three of these had distinctive badges. Badges for the 3rd and 4th Divisional Ammunition Column cap badges[c22] were approved by militia headquarters, but those for the 1st[c23] were not approved. An unapproved badge also was made for the 13th Brigade Ammunition Column.[c24] Under GRO 4663, all artillery units in the field were required to wear the Canada artillery gun cap badge and grenade collar badges.

Trench Mortar Batteries

Attached to each infantry brigade was a Trench Mortar Battery. Two of these in the 4th Division had distinctive badges – the 10th Trench Mortar Battery[c25] and the 11th Trench Mortar Battery[c26]. These were reported by the 4th Division on 27 August 1917 as being used[18] but there is no record of Canadian Corps Headquarters approval. A Trench Mortar Battery cap badge exists of the design illustrated in Cross (150-5-10 & 11), but without a numeral (figure 19). It is unknown if this was a general issue Trench Mortar Battery badge or simply a manufacturer's sample.

Figure 19 Cap badge without Battery numeral

Bob Russell collection

References – Cross' catalogue numbers

c1. 110-1-1

c2. 140-1-2
    140-1-3

c3. 140-1-4
    140-1-5

c4. 140-1-6

c5. 145-3-36

c6. 145-3-56B

c7. 145-3-58

c8. 145-3-50

c9. 145-3-63A

c10.145-3-46
    145-3-64B

c11. 145-3-79B

c12. 145-3-67

c13. 145-3-79A style B

c14. 145-3-13H

c15. 150-1-3A
    150-3-9A
    150-3-9B
    150-1-10

c16. 150-1-4
    150-1-9

c17. 150-1-3B

c18. 150-7-1

c19. 150-1-10

c20. 150-3-5

c21. 150-3-7

c22. 150-9-3
    150-9-4

c23. 150-9-1

c24. 145-3-13A

c25. 150-5-10A
    150-5-10B

c26. 150-5-11

Chapter 4

Line of Communication Units and Other Corps Badges

Cavalry and Mounted Rifles

The Royal Canadian Dragoons and Lord Strathcona's Horse of the Canadian Cavalry Brigade each wore the approved badges of the permanent force.[1] The Fort Garry Horse also was in the Canadian Cavalry Brigade. They were formed in January 1916 from the Canadian Cavalry Depot which had been formed from the 6th Battalion. The badge adopted by the regiment (figure 20) was based on the design of the badge of the 6th Battalion.[2] The regiment had a depot in Winnipeg that supplied reinforcing drafts. The depot was called the 34th Fort Garry Horse, Service Squadron[3] and wore the badges of the parent militia regiment (figure 21).[2]

Each squadron of the Canadian Light Horse was approved to wear the badges of its parent militia regiment i.e., A Squadron, 19th Alberta Dragoons; B Squadron, 1st Hussars; C Squadron, 16th Light Horse.[4] The Royal North West Mounted Police Squadron attached to the Canadian Light Horse and B Squadron RNWMP of the CEF (Siberia) wore the RNWMP badges.[5,c1] However the RNWMP badges were not on the list of badges provided by the Canadian Ordnance Depot under GRO 4663. Unapproved distinctive badges were also used by the Remount Depot[c2] which came under the Canadian Army Service Corps.

The 1st to 13th Regiments, Canadian Mounted Rifles, were placed on active service as of 7 November 1914. All had distinctive badges, but only those for the 6th and 9th CMR were approved. When the 4th CMR requested approval of their badge[c3] they were advised "that special badges for units of the CEF are not permitted". The 7th CMR request for approval of a badge was rejected on the grounds that the design omitted "Overseas". Unapproved badges were in use by the 2nd Canadian Mounted Rifles Brigade[c4] presumably by their HQ staff as the other units in the Brigade had their own badges.

A distinctive badge was used by the Depot Regiment Canadian Mounted Rifles.[c5]

Figure 20 *Cap badge worn by The Fort Garry Horse of the Canadian Cavalry Brigade*

Author's collection

Figure 21 *Cap badge worn by the 34th Fort Garry Horse, Service Squadron in Winnipeg*

Author's collection

Figure 22 *Officers of the 7th Regiment Canadian Mounted Rifles. All but two officers are wearing the rare 7th CMR cap badge (insets) The scrolls read "Gallantry" "Right" "Duty". The fourth officer from the left is wearing the cap badge of the 25th Brant Dragoons. Billy Bishop is wearing the cap badge of the Royal Military College.*

Bob Russell collection

Approval for this badge was requested three times and all applications were denied. There is also a makeshift cap badge known which reads "Overseas Mounted Rifles" (figure 23). It is a badge of the 9th CMR[c6] with a horse's head *dexter* superimposed over the numeral. The Author has not been able to identify the unit that used this badge.[6]

The 1st to 6th Regiments, Canadian Mounted Rifles, were reorganized as infantry battalions on 1 January 1916 and designated the 1st to 4th Canadian Mounted Rifles Battalions, 8th Canadian Infantry Brigade. The other CMR Regiments either reinforced cavalry units or infantry battalions.

Engineers and Pioneers

The Canadian Engineers, CEF used the cap badge of the Corps[c7] in the Canadian Militia that was approved in 1905. Collar badges that were miniatures of the cap badge were also worn, however, grenade collar badges were later approved under GRO 4663.[7]

Figure 23 *Overseas Mounted Rifles makeshift cap badge*

Bob Russell collection

Five Pioneer Battalions were authorized for active service during 1915-16. Each had distinctive badges[c8], but only those for the 2nd, 4th and 5th Pioneer Battalions were approved by militia headquarters. The 1st Pioneer Battalion was originally authorized as the 80th Overseas "Pioneer" Battalion.[8] Jacoby Bros., Vancouver, designed a badge for the newly authorized battalion (figure 25) but it was never produced as the unit was soon redesignated the 1st Canadian Pioneer Battalion.[9] A badge design with this new designation was submitted for approval, but was refused as the word "Overseas" did not appear on the badge. The Battalion went ahead and used the same badge with "Overseas" added.

There is an unapproved badge[c9] which was similar to the design of the 1st Pioneer Battalion but with the number eliminated and the beaver and pick and shovel reversed. It is not clear which units wore this badge. One source states that it was worn by drafts recruited in British Columbia during 1915 to reinforce the 1st Pioneer Battalion; another believes it was the design for the 1st Pioneer Battalion referred to above as having been rejected by militia headquarters.

Five infantry battalions were converted to pioneers. The 48th Battalion became the 3rd Pioneer Battalion in 1916. Their new badge[c10] was never approved. During 1916-17 the other four infantry battalions became the 67th, 107th, 123rd, 124th Pioneer Battalions. They continued to wear their original badges.[c11] All but the 67th

Figure 24 A sapper wearing the 1905 pattern Canadian Engineers cap badge and General Service maple leaf collar badges
Wyn van der Schee collection

Figure 25 Drawing of proposed 80th Pioneer Battalion cap badge
Jacoby Bros files

Figure 26 Capt F G Armitage wearing 5th Pioneer Battalion badges
NAC PA-6838

Battalion's badges had been approved.

The 4th Pioneer Battalion (later renumbered 5th) was absorbed by the Canadian Pioneer Training Depot. Unapproved badges existed for the Depot[c12], also a makeshift pioneers badge (figure 27). By May 1918 the pioneers ceased to exist as such. The 1st Pioneer Battalion became 9th Battalion Canadian Railway Troops. The other battalions either were absorbed by the engineers or used to reinforce infantry battalions.

Figure 27 Makeshift cap badge likely for the Pioneer Depot

Bob Russell collection

Labour Group

The 1st to 4th Canadian Labour Battalions were formed overseas during November 1916 to February 1917. The 4th Canadian Labour Battalion wore unapproved badges.[c13] The other battalions wore the General Service maple leaf badges.[10] The Officers of the 3rd Labour Battalion wore the cap badge of their original unit however.[11]

The 2nd and 3rd Labour Battalions became 12th and 11th Battalions Canadian Railway Troops respectively during November 1917. The 1st and 4th were reorganized during September 1918 as the Canadian Labour Group comprising the 1st to 4th Canadian Infantry Works Companies. Distinctive cap badges [c14] were approved for the four companies.[12] There also were the 1st to 4th Entrenching Battalions in existence between July 1916 and October 1917. These wore either the General Service maple leaf badges or the badges of their original unit.[13]

Signal Service

The Signals Branch CEF was part of the Canadian Engineers CEF and was designated Canadian Signals, Canadian Engineers in June 1917. The Divisional Signal Companies wore engineers badges by August 1917.[14] These were issued by the Canadian Ordnance Depot to units in the field under GRO 4663. Some signal personnel wore the Canadian Signal Corps badges[c15,15] approved in 1908, but this had not been approved for the CEF[16]. However HQ Canadian Corps advised the Director of Ordnance Services September 1917 that:

> The Corps Commander desires that those individual Officers and men who at this date wear the crossed flags badges, and who wish to continue to wear them, shall be allowed to do so, but that all others and all reinforcements to the Signal Companies shall wear the Engineer badges.[17]

Machine Gun Corps

On 15 September 1914 a Machine Gun Corps was authorized, the units of which were to form part of the CEF. The first unit was the Automobile Machine Gun Brigade No 1 (AMGB), followed by Borden's Machine Gun Battery, Eaton's Machine Gun Battery and Boyle's Yukon Machine Gun Detachment. The first badges worn by these units were the

General Service maple leaf badges. Also, at that time each infantry battalion had its own machine gun section which wore the badges of the battalion.

During May 1915 before proceeding to France AMGB No 1 became the 1st Canadian Motor Machine Gun Brigade. Distinctive badges[c16] were introduced in July 1916[18] without militia headquarters approval. Badges were also introduced for Borden's[19,c17] and Eaton's[c18] Batteries and Boyle's Yukon Detachment.[20,c19] Only the badges of Eaton's Machine Gun Battery were approved.

Borden's, Eaton's and Boyle's became Borden, Eaton and Yukon Motor Machine Gun Batteries respectively during 1916. A new cap badge[c20] which was not approved by Canadian Corps Headquarters was introduced for the Eaton Motor Machine Gun Battery, and collar badges worn were those of the British Machine Gun Corps.[21,c21] There is another badge known for the Eaton Motor Machine Gun Battery pictured on the

Figure 28 Charles H Fee, BSM Unit Train (MSM) wearing silver badges of the 1st Canadian Motor Machine Gun Brigade

Courtesy Fee Family

cover of Cross' book on Corps Badges. It is oval and depicts their original armoured cars. There is no information in the unit's files that indicate the origin of this badge and when and how it was used.[22] New badges were also introduced for the Yukon Motor Machine Gun Battery (figure 29)[c22] without approval. These probably were worn only by the Officers.[23] The OC Borden Motor Machine Gun Battery reported June 1917 that "the majority of the men are wearing ordinary Machine Gun Badges".[24]

Figure 29 Cap badge (left) and collar badge (right) of the Yukon Motor Machine Gun Battery. The collar badge is often mistaken for a cap badge.

Ron Edwards photograph and Author's collection

The 86th Battalion was mobilized during 1915 as a Machine Gun Battalion. After arrival overseas they became the Canadian Machine Gun Depot on 22 June 1916. The 86th Battalion badges were eventually replaced by those of the British Machine Gun Corps.[c21]

The 205th Battalion was reorganized in Canada into a draft-giving depot machine gun battalion on 20 December 1916. The 205th reported that they were wearing the 205th Battalion badges[c23] in September 1917 but asked permission to wear CMGC badges instead. It is not known if permission was received. The New Brunswick Machine Gun Draft (1 officer and 41 ORs) authorized 20 September 1916 had an unapproved cap badge and collar badges[c24] that were miniatures of the cap badge.

Figure 30 Collar badge of the 4th Canadian Machine Gun Company

Author's collection

Meanwhile in the UK and France, the machine gun sections in the infantry battalions were formed into Machine Gun Companies serving with their various brigades. Canadian Corps HQ asked the formations in the field to report what badges were being worn by the various units. The three Divisions in the field reported in August 1917 that the 3rd, 4th and 9th Machine Gun Companies had distinctive badges[25,c25]. None of these badges had been approved by Canadian Corps Headquarters. The other Machine Gun Companies wore the cap badge of the British Machine Gun Corps[c21] and the maple leaf collar badges.[26]

The organization of the Canadian Machine Gun Corps in France was approved effective 16 April 1917. In March 1918 the Machine Gun Companies were formed into 1st to 4th Machine Gun Battalions serving with their respective Divisions. The Deputy Adjutant and Quartermaster General advised the machine gun units in the field by ADOS 4/1, 27 October 1917 that the approved badges for the Corps are the cap and collar badges of the British Machine Gun Corps.[27] Canadian Corps RO 1766, 7 May 1918, repeated the contents of the foregoing and further stated:

> Unauthorized badges now worn in the the units of the Canadian Machine Gun Corps should be replaced as soon as possible in accordance with the above (ie ADOS 4/1).

The issuance of GRO 4663, 1 August 1918, confirmed that the British Machine Gun Corps cap badge and General Service maple leaf collar badges were to be worn in the field. This was amended by GRO 4798, 17 August 1918, which approved placing the word CANADA between the butts of the crossed machine guns on the cap and collar badges.[c26] However, it is obvious from photographs that the British Machine Gun Corps badge continued to be worn by some units until after the Armistice.

Tiptafts also produced special maple leaf design cap and collar badges[c27] worn for a time in England and others shipped to Calais, France.[28] These were returned because "GHQ will not sanction the wearing of these badges cap (sic) of incorrect pattern".[29] These badges were also worn for a time by the Canadian Machine Gun Depot at Seaford.[30] Collars of this pattern appear to have been widely worn, however. Photographs also show these collars worn by some members of the 2nd Canadian Motor Machine Gun Brigade and the 2nd Machine Gun Battalion. An unusual Canadian Machine Gun Corps cap badge (likely an officer's cap badge) also exists.[31]

On 19 September 1918 1st Canadian Motor Machine Gun Brigade was granted permission to wear the original collar badges of the Automobile Machine Gun Brigade No l to be worn with the "MGC Crossed Guns and Crown" cap badge.[32] However, a picture of a NCO of the unit shows him wearing the unapproved Canadian Machine Gun Corps maple leaf design collar badges.[c27] An unusual officer's cap badge of the 1st Canadian Motor Machine Gun Brigade has recently appeared in an auction.[33]

Figure 31 One of the types of cap and collar badges and shoulder titles worn in the Canadian Machine Gun Corps

Charles Hamilton collection

References – Cross' catalogue numbers

c1. 10-5-1	c11. 67A	c19. 50-3-5 (maple leaf
c2. 95-15-1	70-3-107	design for both cap
c3. 10-7-4B	70-3-123A	and collar badges)
c4. 10-3-1	70-3-124	c20. 50-3-3
c5. 10-9-1	c12. 70-7-1	c21. 45-1-1
c6. 10-7-9	c13. 70-9-4	c22. 50-3-5 (crossed
c7. 70-1-1	c14. 70-13-1	MG design)
c8. 70-3-1	70-13-2	c23. 205
70-3-2	70-13-3	c24. 45-5-1
70-3-3	70-13-4	c25. 45-3-3
70-3-4	c15. 100-1-1	45-3-4
70-3-5	c16. 50-1-1	45-3-9
c9. 70-5-1	c17. 50-1-3	c26. 45-1-3
c10. 70-3-3	c18. 50-3-1	45-1-5
		45-1-7
		c27. 45-1-9

Chapter 5

More Badges for Line of Communication Troops and Other Corps

Service Corps

The Corps badge approved in 1908 for the permanent force and militia[c1] was worn as allowed by Dress Regulations for Canadian Units, December 1916. Under GRO 4663 these were supplied by the Canadian Ordnance Depot to units in the field. Some of the Service Corps units in the field had distinctive badges, none of which were approved. These were the 1st to 4th Ammunition Sub Parks, Ammunition Sub Park Mechanical Transport Company and the 4th Divisional Train.[c2] By the summer of 1917 the officers of some of the units in the field (including the 4th Divisional Train) were wearing CASC badges and Other Ranks the General Service maple leaf badges.[1] There also were unapproved distinctive badges for "7 Co CASC Winnipeg"[2,c3], No 8 'Overseas' Depot Unit of Supply[c4], and No 1 Overseas Army Service Corps Training Depot[c5]. 19th Company CASC was placed on active service during August 1914 and Jacoby Bros., designed a distinctive cap badge (figure 32). It is likely the badge was never made, although the company had a distinctive shoulder title. Distinctive badges were also made for the Remount Depot which provided horses to the Cavalry.

For some unknown reason, CEF (Canada) RO 492, 26 April 1918 directed that the Service Corps in Canada wear the General Service maple leaf cap badge with the Corps collar badges. All MDs were advised 7 May 1918 by the Director General Supplies and Transport that RO 492 was to be complied with.[3]

Figure 32 Drawing of proposed cap badge for 19th Company CASC

Jacoby Bros files

Medical Services

In May 1909 the medical component of the permanent force and the militia were designated Canadian Army Medical Corps. Medical units were mobilized for the CEF and, at an unknown date[4], the badge[c6] patterned after the Royal Army Medical Corps was introduced in the CEF. Its use was officially acknowledged in the December 1916 CEF Dress Regulations. A few medical units had distinctive badges:

> No 1 Field Ambulance (cap badge only)[c7]
> No 2 Field Ambulance[c8]
> No 4 Field Ambulance[c9]
> No 8 Field Ambulance[c10]
> No 15 (Queen's University) Field Ambulance[5][c11]
> No 7 (Dalhousie University) Stationary Hospital (collar badge only)[6]
> No 8 Stationary Hospital[c12]
> No 9 (St Francis Xavier College) Stationary Hospital[c13]

The badge for No 9 Stationary Hospital was the only badge approved by militia headquarters. The OC No 15 Field Ambulance claimed that their badges were approved by Headquarters in Ottawa, but there was no record of this approval on file. No 1 Field Ambulance cap badge was custom-made and probably worn by only a few of the personnel.[7] The other units in the field wore various combinations of the CAMC badge and the General Service maple leaf badge (Appendix 12). A sweetheart pin exists for No 9 Field Ambulance.[8]

Chaplain Service

Canadian Chaplains in the CEF initially wore the Maltese cross badge approved in 1905 which was that of the Imperial Chaplains.[c14] This was confirmed in the 1916 Dress Regulations.[9] The unapproved variations with a maple leaf in each of the blades of the cross[10,c15] and with a square style cross[c16] and a makeshift cap badge[11] were also worn.

When sending samples of their badges to the Historical Section, Canadian War Records Office, the Director of Chaplain Services expressed their dissatisfaction with the badges in use:

> It is, however, suggested that the huge size of the Cross compared with that of the Crown on the badge is meant to be none too kind or too subtle a reminder of the usual lot of the Chaplain in Service. As to the buttons, the absence of all design or symbolism is too obvious for remarks. Neither, badge, button or shoulder strap is popular in the Service.[12]

The Chaplains in the CEF were formed as the Canadian Chaplain Service on 15 March 1917. The Director of Chaplain Services advised the Director of Ordnance Services on 14 August 1918 that badges would be ordered[13] and the design of new badges[c17] was approved in October.

Military Police

A small group of military police (2 Officers and 11 Other Ranks) sailed for the UK on 3 October 1914 with the 1st Canadian Contingent. Likely they wore the General Service maple leaf badges. At an unknown date the Military Police overseas began wearing badges[c18] partly patterned after the Corps of Military Police of the British Army. This was unauthorized, especially with the Royal cypher which required Royal assent.

On 15 September 1917 the formation of the "Military Police CEF" was authorized with militia headquarters and detachments in each MD in Canada. No 1 Detachment, London, Ontario had a distinctive cap badge.[c19] There also was a cap badge for the Provost Marshal Staff, MD No 10.[14] Neither of these badges was approved. The Canadian Military Police Corps was authorized 1 April 1918 to be formed from the Military Police, CEF. A new cap badge[c20] and collar badge were approved for the Corps the following month. The collar badge consisted of the initials C.M.P.C. which may be mistaken for a shoulder title. The initials C.M.P were initially recommended as the collar badge and the Author has seen a picture of these being worn as well. The approved shoulder title was the plain Canada title.

Corps Cyclists

The Corps Cyclists originally comprised four Divisional Cyclist Companies and a Canadian Reserve Cyclist Company, each having distinctive badges. The badges of the 2nd Divisional Cyclist Company[c21] and the 3rd Divisional Cyclist Company[c22] were approved by militia headquarters. There also is a makeshift badge known for the 2nd Divisional Cyclist Company.[c23] The badges worn by the 1st Divisional Cyclist Company[c24], the 4th Divisional Cyclist Company[c25] and the 5th Divisional Cyclist Company[15,c26] were not approved.

In May 1916 the Canadian Corps Cyclist Battalion was formed to replace the divisional cyclist companies. Its badges[c27] were based on the design of the British Army Cyclist Corps badge and were approved in December 1917. There were a number of cyclist platoons formed to provide reinforcing drafts to the Canadian Corps Cyclist Battalion. An unapproved badge[c28] was worn by some of the officers of these platoons.

Forestry Corps

The roots of the Canadian Forestry Corps CEF were the 224th and 238th Canadian Forestry Battalions formed during 1916. Both had approved distinctive badges.[c29] The 224th arrived in the UK in four parties during May/June 1916. The parties were sent to various areas of the UK to cut timber. Cap badges of the 224th exist with the numeral "1" or "2" superimposed over the numerals 224.[c30] It is not clear which units wore these badges.[16] The 238th arrived in the UK in September 1916 and on 14 November it was amalgamated with the 224th to form the Canadian Forestry Corps. Two General Service Forestry Corps badges were in use during 1916-18, both of which were unapproved. One was the approved design of the badge of the 230th Forestry Battalion with numbers removed[c31] made by Hemsleys in Montreal; the other the approved design of the 238th Forestry Battalion also with the numbers removed[c32] made by Tiptafts in Birmingham. These badges were not supplied through the Canadian Ordnance Depot. It is not known which units used these badges. It was not until June 1918 that Corps badges[c33] were approved.

After the Corps was formed, the 230th and 242nd Forestry Battalions and the 122nd Battalion[17] arrived from Canada and were absorbed into the Corps. Over one-half of the 165th Battalion from the 13th Reserve Battalion was absorbed as well. These battalions all had approved badges.[c34]

One hundred and two forestry companies were formed overseas. By the time of the armistice, fifty-six were serving in the war zone. Distinctive badges are known for Nos 12, 50 and 70 Forestry Companies.[c35] All were made by Tiptafts but none was approved by OMFC Headquarters.

During 1917 Depots, Companies and Drafts were authorized in each MD in Canada. There were several badges in use that likely were used by these units. These were:

> *Military District No 2*
> Badge device, Forestry Draft York and Simcoe Counties (figure 33).[18]
> *Military Districts Nos 4 & 5*
> Cap badge, Les Forestiers de Quebec.[c36]

Military District No 6

Cap badge, 230th Battalion badge with N.B overlaid on the number[c37]

Badges, 238th Battalion badge with N.B overlaid on the number[c38]

Cap Badge,230th Battalion badge with N.S overlaid on the number (figure 34)

Badges, 238th Battalion badge with N.S overlaid on the number[c39]

Military District No 10

Badges, Forestry Company M D No 10[c40]

Military District No 11

Cap badge, 238th Battalion badge design with the number removed, in smaller size, made by O B Allen, Vancouver[c41]

Figure 33 *Forestry Draft York and Simcoe Counties badge device*

Author's collection

Figure 34 *Nova Scotia Forestry Draft/Depot cap badge*

Author's collection

Only the badge of the Winnipeg Forestry Company was approved by militia headquarters. It is not known which of the badges in MD Nos 4, 5, 6 and 11 were used by the various units formed in these Districts. The units are listed in Appendix 13. The Author would be pleased to hear of any photographic evidence that would identify the units wearing these badges.

Railway Troops

The Canadian Railway Construction Corps was raised during the spring of 1915 and sailed for the UK on 14 June. Distinctive badges were used by the Corps[c42] but were never approved by militia headquarters. After the formation of the Corps, two construction battalions and six railway construction battalions arrived in the UK between September and March 1917. All had their own badge approved by militia headquarters:

Figure 35 *A soldier wearing the 239th Railway Construction Battalion cap badge*

Wyn van der Schee collection

No 1 Construction Battalion[c43]
No 2 Construction Battalion[c44]
143rd Railway Construction Battalion[c45]
218th Railway Construction Battalion[c46]
228th Railway Construction Battalion[c47]
239th Railway Construction Battalion[c48]
256th Overseas Railway Construction Battalion[c49]
257th Overseas Railway Construction Battalion[c50]

An unusual officer's cap badge of No 1 Construction Battalion recently was offered in auction.[19] Also an unusual variety of 256th Battalion cap badge exists (figure 36). The Railway Construction Depot did not appear to have a distinctive badge, but a distinctive sweetheart pin for the depot is known.[20]

Figure 36 256th Battalion makeshift cap badge

Bob Russell collection

Nos 1 to 3 Sections Skilled Railway Employees were formed in 1917.[21] All had their own badges[c51] but only those for No 1 Section[c52] were approved by militia headquarters. The Sections later became known as 58th Broad Gauge Railway Operating Company, 13th Light Operating Company and 69th Wagon Erecting Company respectively.

After the commencement of the engagements at the Somme it was decided to make greater use of railways in the forward areas of the front. Canada agreed to provide five battalions of Railway Troops. Between late November 1916 and early February 1917, No 1 Construction Battalion, 127th Battalion and 239th Overseas Railway Construction Battalion were converted to 1st, 2nd, 3rd Battalions Canadian Railway Troops. The 4th and 5th Battalions Canadian Railway Troops (CRT) were formed at Purfleet in the UK. The 2nd Battalion CRT continued to use the 127th Battalion's approved badges, but distinctive badges were introduced for the other four battalions.[c53]

It was decided to increase the number of battalions and as more units arrived from Canada they were sent to the CRT Depot at Purfleet. The 6th to 13th Battalions CRT were formed, mostly by conversion of existing units:

6th Battalion Canadian Railway Troops[c54]
(formerly 228th Railway Construction Battalion)
7th Battalion Canadian Railway Troops[22,c55]
(formerly 257th Overseas Railway Construction Battalion)
8th Battalion Canadian Railway Troops[c56]
(formed from the majority of the 211th Battalion and 218th Railway Construction Battalion)
9th Battalion Canadian Railway Troops (1st Pioneer Battalion badges[c57])
(formerly 1st Pioneer Battalion)
10th Battalion Canadian Railway Troops[c58]
(formerly 256th Overseas Railway Construction Battalion)
11th Battalion Canadian Railway Troops[c59]
(formerly 3rd Canadian Labour Battalion)
12th Battalion Canadian Railway Troops[c60]
(formerly 2nd Canadian Labour Battalion)
13th Battalion Canadian Railway Troops[c61] (formed at Purfleet)

All but the 9th Battalion CRT introduced distinctive badges. Unapproved badges also are known for the Canadian Railway Troops Depot in Canada.[23,c62] Upon the 239th Battalion being redesignated the 3rd Battalion Canadian Railway Troops, a makeshift cap badge was created by cutting out the 2 and 9 from the 239th badge.[24,c63] An unusual 4th Battalion CRT cap badge exists (figure 38).[25] Two makeshift badges are known for the 10th Battalion CRT. One is the 256th Battalion badge with the numeral 10 overlaid on the battalion number,[c64] the other, found in the Canadian War Museum collection, is a 10th Battalion CRT collar badge mounted on the General Service maple leaf cap badge.[c65]

***Figure 37** 7th CRT cap badge, 1st issue*
Author's collection

Nothing could be found in the files of HQ OMFC or HQ CRT, Purfleet, showing that any of the distinctive badges used by the CRT Battalions and the Depot had been approved. Reference to badges was found in Canadian Railway Troops RO 71, 9 June 1917 which stated:

> Further to the Order that Battalions may wear badges of their original formation, not more than one style of badge is permitted in a Battalion. A Battalion wearing its own distinctive badge must provide itself with a sufficient supply to fully equip its personnel.

***Figure 38** 4th CRT unusual cap badge*
Bob Russell collection

HQ OMFC did request specimens of badges worn by the Battalions and these were sent to militia headquarters in Ottawa January 1918 and afterwards.[26] All the battalions except the 7th served outside the Canadian Corps in British Army formations, so it is possible the badges were approved by a higher authority in the British Army.[27]

The Corps of Canadian Railway Troops were authorized on 23 April 1918. It comprised the thirteen CRT battalions, four CRT companies and the CRT depot and also absorbed the Canadian Railway Construction Corps. No 2 Construction Battalion had been transferred to the Canadian Forestry Corps.

The Corps formed the 1st Bridging Company in August/September 1918 to serve in Palestine in General Allenby's Egyptian Expeditionary Force. It had distinctive badges[c66] but there is no record of approval.

When it was announced 27 October 1917 that badges would be supplied by the Canadian Ordnance Depot from public funds, the Canadian railway troops units were not included.[28] The Director of Ordnance Services stated on 6 June 1918:

. . . the amount of money voted for the purpose of buying these Badges was very limited and we are endeavouring to do the best we can with the money available . . . It is not proposed to supply them for Canadian Pioneer Battalions or Canadian Railway Troops . . . neither is it intended to supply to the other Units, such as the Engine Crew Company, etc., mentioned in your list, as we have not knowledge of any of these badges being authorized or applied for . . . [29]

CRT cap badge

CRT collar badge

Figure 39 *Drawing of CRT badges approved but never made NAC C-1013-33*

However on 3 October the Corps GOC put forth a proposal "that a Corps badge be authorized . . . that such badge be issued free of cost to all Other Ranks in the Corps CRT".[30] In submitting the proposal to HQ OMFC the GOC Canadian Section GHQ wrote on 21 October 1918:

> At present these units are wearing various badges which have been supplied from private sources, and is now considered desirable, in order to foster the esprit de corps of Canadian Railway Units as a whole that they should all wear the same badge.[31]

The design of the badges (figure 39) was approved 28 October 1918, but the war ended 11 November and the badges were never made.

Tank Corps

The new war machine, the tank, made its debut 15 September 1916 at the Somme. British Army tanks supported the Canadian Corps. It was not until 1918 that the 1st and 2nd Tank Battalions were formed in the CEF as units of the Canadian Machine Gun Corps. The badges for the 1st Tank Battalion[c67] were approved by militia headquarters. There also is an unusual badge known for the 1st Tank Battalion (figure 40). A cap badge for the 2nd Tank Battalion[32] was made by overlaying 2nd on the numeral of the 1st Tank Battalion badge. There is no record of approval for this modification. It may have been a prototype.

Figure 40 *Makeshift cap badge 1st Tank Battalion*

Bob Russell collection

During November 1918 the Canadian Tank Corps CEF was formed and the 1st and 2nd Tank Battalions became units of the Corps. The Corps was also given authority to form additional battalions. As a result the 3rd Tank Battalion was authorized. A few prototype badges[c68] were hand-made. A cap badge for the Canadian Tank Corps[c69] was approved after the armistice. A makeshift badge for the Corps also is known.[33]

References - Cross' catalogue numbers

c1. 95-1-1	c13. 85-3-9	c30. 30-5-1	c42. 65-1-1	c54. 65-5-6A
c2. 95-5-1	c14. 80-1-3	30-5-2	c43. 65-3-1	65-5-6B
95-5-2	c15. 80-1-5	c31. 30-3-3	c44. 65-3-2	c55. 65-5-7B 2nd issue
95-5-3	c16. 80-1-7	c32. 30-3-1	c45. 143	c56. 65-5-8
95-5-4	c17. 80-1-1	c33. 30-1-1A	c46. 218	c57. 70-3-1
95-7-4	c18. 60-1-1B	c34. 230B	c47. 228	c58. 65-5-10C
95-9-1*	c19. 60-3-1	242	c48. 239	c59. 65-5-11
c3. 95-3-7	c20. 60-1-1A	122A	c49. 256	c60. 65-5-12
c4. 95-13-8‡	c21. 20-3-2A	165	c50. 257A	c61. 65-5-13
c5. 95-17-1	c22. 20-3-3	c35. 30-5-12	257B	c62. 65-7-1
c6. 85-1-1	c23. 20-3-2B	30-5-50	c51. 65-11-1	c63. 65-3-3B
c7. 85-7-1	c24. 20-3-1	30-5-70	65-11-2	c64. 65-5-10B
c8. 85-7-2C	c25. 20-3-4	c36. 30-5-90	65-11-3	c65. 65-5-10D
c9. 85-7-4	c26. 20-3-5	c37. 30-5-86	c52. 65-11-1	c66. 65-9-1
c10. 85-7-8	c27. 20-1-1	c38. 30-5-84	c53. 65-5-1	c67. 75-3-1
c11. 85-7-2A	c28. 20-5-1	c39. 30-5-88	65-5-3	c68. 75-3-3
85-7-2B	c29. 30-3-4	c40. 30-5-82	65-5-4	c69. 75-1-1A
c12. 85-3-8	30-3-5	c41. 30-3-1 small	65-5-5A	

*Truck design collar badges are illustrated in Jeffrey Hoare Sale 58, Feb 1998, Item 2588.

‡Collar badges are illustrated in Jeffrey Hoare Sale 58, Feb 1998, Item 2593.

Chapter 6

Badges of Other Services, Units and Organizations

Dental Services

The Canadian Army Dental Corps was authorized 20 April 1915 and personnel began arriving in the UK for the CEF during the following July. The first issue of badges[c1] contained the letters DS for Dental Service. It is not known if they had been approved. However the badge design was amended[c2] to contain the letters OS, for overseas. It was approved by militia headquarters.

Ordnance Services

The permanent force Canadian Ordnance Corps contingent sailed for the UK with the 1st Contingent on 3 October 1914. The Corps established depots and service units in the UK and France. The badges of the Corps approved in 1904[c3] were worn in the CEF. The Canadian Arms Inspection and Repair Department was authorized July 1916 and located in London, England also had distinctive badges[c4] which were approved.

Veterinary Services

Detachments from the permanent force and militia Canadian Army Veterinary Corps arrived at Valcartier for the CEF during August 1914. As the number of horses in the CEF increased, additional Veterinary Sections were formed and sailed for service overseas and HQ CAVC Overseas was established. The first badges worn were those approved for the Corps in 1912.[c5] A new badge for the CAVC Overseas[c6] was approved and supplies were ordered February 1916 for delivery to the Canadian Ordnance Depot at Ashford.[1]

Pay Services

Following the outbreak of war, the Canadian Army Pay Corps of the permanent force provide a small number of paymasters and cashiers to the CEF. Initially they would have worn overseas the Corps badges approved in 1905[c7]. Other pay personnel likely wore either the General Service maple leaf badges or those of their unit. In October 1916 the formation of the Canadian Army Pay Corps CEF was authorized comprising the pay personnel at all levels. The Corps establishment was authorized in April 1917. The design of badges[c8] for the new Corps was

Figure 41 Captain C French wearing the 1912 pattern Canadian Veterinary Corps badges.
National Archives of Canada PA 7220

immediately submitted[2] and their use was approved in CAPC Dress Regulations.[3]

Postal Service

One of the first arrivals in Valcartier in August 1914 for the 1st Contingent was a militia detachment of the Canadian Postal Corps. As the war progressed the Corps provided army post offices in the UK and France. Initially these units wore the Corps badge approved in 1912.[4,c9] It was reported in May 1917, however, that the postal units were wearing the General Service maple leaf badges.[4] This was obviously a temporary situation as a supply was shipped from Tiptafts to the Canadian Ordnance Depot on 16 December 1918.[6]

General Headquarters Staff

The Canadian War Records Office received specimens of the cap badges and shoulder titles worn by General Headquarters Staff.[7] The badges were those worn by the British, the Royal cypher GRV surmounted by a crown.[8] However, in his October 1917 Report the Director of Personal Services wrote:

> Shorncliffe informed that the wearing of "GR" badge in OMFC is not authorized, but that Headquarters Sub Staff should wear the universal Maple Leaf Badge and Other Ranks attached to it, these Sub Staffs should wear badge of their own unit.[9]

A distinctive Canadian General Headquarters badge recently appeared in an auction.[10] There also was a Canadian Military Headquarters badge.[c10] It has not been established if this latter badge was worn in the CEF.

Military Staff Clerks

A Detachment of the Corps of Military Staff Clerks, CEF was formed in each of the eleven Military Districts in Canada. They wore the badges of the Corps[c11] approved in 1908. But it has not been established if members of the Corps serving at GHQ in London, England wore the badges of the Corps.[11]

Musketry Training

In August 1914 the staff of the Canadian School of Musketry (Permanent Force) went to Valcartier to train the 1st Contingent. They would have worn the badges of the school approved in 1912.[c12] During November 1916 the Canadian School of Musketry CEF was opened in the UK. It is uncertain whether this latter school wore the badges of the permanent force school in Canada or the General Service maple leaf badges.[12]

Gymnastic Staff

The Canadian Army Gymnastic Staff CEF provided the troops in Canada and overseas with instructors in bayonet fighting and physical training. A School of Bayonet Fighting and Physical Training was authorized 1 February 1916. The cap badge[c13] worn by the staff was approved for wear with the General Service maple leaf collars. Collar badges of the cap badge design are known but they were not approved for wear. Instructors in bayonet fighting and physical training on the subordinate staff of the Military Districts in Canada were approved to wear crossed-swords without a crown as their cap badge.

General Auditor

The Department of the General Auditor CEF was authorized September 1916 to audit the financial records and transactions of the CEF. They were located in London, England. Personnel wore distinctive badges[c14] which were approved by HQ OMFC.

Corps of Guides

Units of the Corps of Guides were not called out for active service with the 1st Contingent, but some 235 men arrived at Valcartier as volunteers. When they arrived they probably wore the badges of the Corps approved in 1904.[c15] However these badges likely would have been replaced by General Service maple leaf badges in Valcartier or by those of their new unit after arriving in the UK. It is doubtful if the Corps badge was worn in the CEF overseas.[11]

Valcartier Camp

Units of the 1st Contingent were concentrated and trained at Valcartier, Quebec during August and September 1914. The lands at Valcartier recently had been acquired by the Militia Department and the site was chosen as the camp for the muster of the contingent. Construction began in early August. Afterwards it served as the training camp for most of the CEF units raised in MD Nos 4, 5 and 6 (Quebec and the Maritimes). A distinctive badge (figure 42)[13] for the Staff exists which was not approved.

Figure 42 *Badge Valcartier Camp Staff*

Author's collection

Guard Duty in Canada

The Railway Service Guards were formed in 1915 to escort Chinese labour personnel from the west coast to the eastern seaboard.[14] They had distinctive badges[c16] which were not approved. A version of the cap badge with 12 mounted thereon (presumably standing for MD No 12) appeared in a 1992 auction.[15]

Eleven Special Service Companies were formed in 1917 to provide guards at military installations and strategic points in Canada. Nos 2, 3 and 12 Special Service Companies had a distinctive cap badge, No 2 Special Service Company wore the General Service maple leaf collar badges.[16, c17] A cap badge of No 6 Special Service Company recently appeared in an auction.[17] None of the cap badges was approved by militia headquarters. The other companies likely wore General Service maple leaf cap and collar badges.

In April 1918 the Canadian Garrison Regiment, eleven battalions, was authorized to absorb the Special Service Companies on its formation. A distinctive badge for the Regiment[c18] was approved by militia headquarters. A specimen exists of the 4th Battalion badge[c19], but approval of it was rejected. It is not known if this ever was worn. The 6th Battalion also proposed distinctive badges but approval was not given. The 11th Battalion in British Columbia wore its own badges[c20] which were not approved.

Khaki University

On 19 September 1918 authority was received for HQ OMFC to establish the Khaki University of Canada with personnel to be drawn from the CEF. Its role was to re-educate the troops during the period of demobilization. Distinctive badges[c21] were approved for wear by the personnel of the university.

Canadian Military YMCA

The Canadian Military YMCA in France was a unit of the OMFC with an establishment of Officers and men. Most of its work was within the Canadian Corps. The unit had distinctive badges[c22] which were not approved.

Field Comforts Commission

This was a military organization founded by a group of Canadian women for the distribution of gifts and voluntary supplies to the troops of the CEF. It was formed at Valcartier in September 1914 and went overseas the following month. Staff and facilities were provided by the OMFC. Staff wore a cap badge[c23] which was not approved. It was a General Service maple leaf cap badge with the letters FCC mounted thereon. A badge (figure 43) also existed for the Auxiliary.[18]

UNITS AND ORGANIZATIONS OUTSIDE THE CEF

Figure 43 Badge of the FCC Auxiliary

Bob Russell collection

There were other units and organizations raised during 1914-19 as part of the country's war effort. Some of these had distinctive badges and some collectors believe they are CEF badges. These units were not part of the CEF but they were a valuable part of the war effort. It is the Author's belief that it would be worthwhile to describe those units and their badges so one would clearly understand "those that are not CEF badges".

Knights of Columbus Catholic Army Huts

These were formed and financed by the Knights of Columbus to provide chapels for catholic soldiers and social and recreational facilities for all troops regardless of creed in the UK and at the front. A cap badge is known for this organization (figure 44).

Canadian Salvation Army

The Canadian Salvation Army, in conjunction with its British counterpart, provided huts and padres for soldiers of the CEF in the UK and France. Members wore the badges of "the Army".[c24] The cap badge was 2" x 2" in size.

Figure 44 Cap badge Knights of Columbus Catholic Army Huts

Bob Russell collection

Soldiers' Rehabilitation

The Department of Soldiers' Civil Re-establishment worked closely with the CEF to assist its personnel on their return to civilian life. The Department had a distinctive cap badge (figure 45).[19]

British Columbia Aviation Units

Two aviation units were formed in British Columbia during the war. The Aviation Corps had distinctive badges (figure 46) and the British Columbia Aviation School distinctive collar badges (figure 47)[20].

Figure 45 Cap badge Department of Soldiers' Civil Re-establishment

Author's collection

Figure 47 British Columbia Aviation School collar badge

Author's collection

Figure 46 Aviation Corps cap badge

late CB Hill-Tout collection

Imperial Munitions Board

The Imperial Munitions Board issued a badge[c25] to women munitions workers in Canada. The badge was given after thirty days employment, and a service bar was added for each six months of continuous work at one plant.[21]

Home Guard/Reserve Militia

After war was declared there was a surge of patriotic feelings. Home Guard units began organizing through civilian initiatives across the country. Some of the earliest units were formed in Portage la Prairie, Toronto, Hamilton and Montreal.[22] The Home Guards were voluntary civilian units although they were encouraged by the military authorities. Once fully organized some of the units began pressing for official status. Thus the Reserve Militia was authorized 15 June 1915 and regulations published. Some of the Home Guard units were enrolled in the Reserve Militia and additional units formed during 1916-17. A few of these units had distinctive badges although none were approved officially:

Toronto Home Guard[23]	cap and collar badges[b1]
	metal title TORONTO[24]
Montreal Home Guard[25]	cap badge[b2]
	metal title M.H.G. (on a plate)

United Farmers of Alberta
  Mounted Infantry Corps[26]   cap and collar badges[b3]
1st Winnipeg Infantry Regiment
  Reserve Militia[27]   collar badge[b4]
Deloraine Reserve Militia
  Battalion[28]   cap badge (figure 48)

A title A.H.G and a cap badge QHG[29] are also known to exist. They probably were used by a Home Guard unit that has not been identified. The Edmonton Home Guard Battalion[30] wore a lapel button for identification.[31]

Women's Volunteer Reserve

This unit initially was formed in Edmonton during July 1915 to do military drill, first aid, nursing, ambulance work and signalling.[32] The unit also had a band. Badges (figure 49) are known for this unit, the cap badge and shoulder title bearing the name of

Figure 48 Deloraine Reserve Militia cap badge
Author's collection

their Edmonton maker, Jackson Bros. The Winnipeg Women's Volunteer Reserve was formed the following month. In addition to military training the unit was involved in other war and charitable work. The Winnipeg reserve wore the title WWVR as a hat badge.[33]

Figure 49 Women's Volunteer Reserve Edmonton cap and collar badge and shoulder title
Author's collection

References - Babin's and Cross' catalogue numbers

Babin	Cross			
b1. 42-1	c1. 105-1-1A	c11. 15-3-	c19. 35-5-4	
b2. 42-2	c2. 105-1-1B	c12. 15-7-1	c20. 35-3-1	
b3. 42-5	c3. 125-1-1	c13. 15-7-3	c21. 165-1-1	
b4. 38-9	c4. 125-3-1	c14. 5-5-1	c22. 55-1-1	
	c5. 5-1-3A	c15. 40-1-1	55-1-3	
	5-1-3B	c16. 60-5-4	55-1-5	
	c6. 5-1-1	c17. 60-5-2A	c23. 155-1-1	
	c7. 90-1-1	60-5-2B	c24. 80-3-1	
	c8. 90-1-3	60-5-3	80-3-3	
	c9. 130-1-1	60-5-12	c25. 160-1-1	
	c10. 15-1-1	c18. 35-1-1		

Chapter 7

Shoulder Titles

Early in the War

At the outbreak of the war the Ordnance Stores had been issuing metal titles to the Royal Canadian Dragoons, Royal Canadian Horse Artillery, Canadian Field Artillery, Canadian Garrison Artillery and the Royal Canadian Regiment. These were brass titles with large 11/16" letters - RCD, RCHA, CFA, CGA, RCR. Likely these were worn when the units were first placed on active service. Later (probably during 1915) the titles were made in bronze with 1/2" size letters with periods after the letters except for the last letter. It is known that early in the life of some of the infantry battalions of the 1st Contingent embroidered cloth shoulder titles were worn.[1] Probably these were used for only a very short time.

The Minister of Militia proposed on 9 December 1914 that the following metal titles for the shoulder straps be used: "add above CANADA the unit designation such as 21-INF, 3 C.F.A., 2 A.M.B."[2] The CANADA title, numerals and initials were approved for the CEF by MO 164, 29 March 1915.[3] The Canadian Ordnance Depot in the UK was notified by Colonel Carson (the Minister of Militia's representative in the UK) on 21 April 1915 that:

> . . . as far as our 1st Division is concerned, I ordered shoulder numerals for them from Elkingtons at the request of General Alderson on a pattern approved by him".[4]

Practices and Directives in Canada

During 1915-16 many new units were being mobilized in Canada. Militia Order (MO) 164/1915, had stated, rather vaguely, that the approved shoulder titles in the issue of "necessaries" in the CEF were "Canada, prs; Initials, sets; Numerals, sets". However, some units were introducing titles and/or initials which the authorities considered unapproved. Accordingly MO 171, 1 May 1916 was issued:

> Attention has been called to the fact that certain Units being mobilized in Canada, are using brass lettering on the men's shoulder straps, which have not been authorized by Militia Headquarters. No groups of letters are to be used in this connection without the authority of Militia Headquarters.

There even seemed to be some confusion about the CANADA title. The Quartermaster General issued a circular letter during June 1916 stating that:

> . . . all members of the Canadian Expeditionary Force should wear the title "CANADA" on the Shoulder Straps of Jacket. These Shoulder Titles are a free issue on demand to NCO's and men and will be provided by Officers out of their outfit allowance.[5]

Practices and Directives Overseas

1st Division RO 1378, 8 November 1915 ordered 1st Division units to wear only the CANADA title on the shoulder straps of the service jacket. The NCO's and men of some of the units began wearing the maple leaf badge on the shoulder straps of jackets and great coats. CTD DO 198 issued 14 January 1916 stated this ". . . is unauthorized and the practice must cease".

On 25 May 1916 the Chief Ordnance Officer CEF in the UK listed the titles which were being supplied to units in the UK and France as being:[6]

(3) Badges shoulder strap:
(a) CANADA
(b) Canadian A.S.C.
(c) Canadian Garrison Artillery
(d) "SIGNAL" (for divisional signal units)
(e) "INF" (for infantry battalions)
(f) Numeral "12" (for Inf Battalions, all numbers are supplied to correspond with the number of the Batn)
(3):- (a) This badge should be worn by all units of the Canadian Expeditionary Force.
(b) (c) and (d), are applicable to the arm of the service mentioned.
(e) and (f). For Infantry Battalions only. The badges worn on shoulder straps of Infantry units are placed in the following order points:-

12
INF
Canada

Major General Arthur Currie, OC 1st Canadian Division wrote to Canadian Corps HQ 29 July 1916 raising the following points:

With regard to the shoulder badges, I think units such as the Royal Highlanders of Canada (13th Bn), the Royal Montreal Regiment (14th Bn), and the Canadian Scottish (16th Bn) should wear those names on their shoulder straps in place of the word Canada.[7]

Dress Regulations for Canadian Units were authorized December 1916 which specified the approved titles to be worn on the shoulder straps above the CANADA title. For infantry and artillery units they were to be the battalion number and INF, battery number and CFA, RCHA or SA[8]. For the corps and services they were SIGNAL, CASC, CAMC, CAVC, COC, CADC, CMFP, CMMP. In practice most of these units wore only one title, the Corps title or the CANADA title.

The A/Adjutant-General of the Canadian Militia in Ottawa was concerned about the use of cloth shoulder titles. He stated in a letter to HQ in London on 3 May 1917:

. . . information has been received that certain Units proceeding Overseas are wearing a red shoulder title on the sleeve with the word CANADA or CYCLIST in white letters. The use of this distinction by any other Battalion than the

Princess Patricia's Canadian Light Infantry is unauthorized and should be discontinued.[9]

Headquarters Canadians Routine Orders (CRO) 1678, 12 June 1917 confirmed the above. On 14 September 1917 CRO 2467 was also issued regarding the wearing of CANADA on the shoulder straps:

> All Officers and Other Ranks of the Overseas Military Forces of Canada will wear the title "Canada" on their shoulder straps as follows:
> Officers wearing metal rank badges on their shoulder straps will wear a metal "Canada" in 3/8" in depth; the metal being either bass or bronze, according to rank badge.
> Officers wearing worsted rank badges on their shoulder straps will wear a worsted "Canada" 3/8" in depth.
> Officers wearing rank badges on their sleeves may wear either brass or worsted "Canada" on their shoulder straps.
> Other Ranks will wear the "Canada" badge as issued by the Ordnance Department.

Later CRO 2683, 18 October 1917 stated that the "last paragraph (CRO 2467) will not apply to units who wear an approved regimental badge on shoulder straps".

Figure 50 *Some different types of Canada titles (reduced)*

Author's collection

Policy on Titles Established

After discussions in Ottawa it was decided that shoulder titles along with badges would be provided to units in the field at public expense. A directive on this policy dated 27 October 1917 was sent to all formations in the field.[10] This policy was published in GRO 4663 which listed the shoulder titles to be provided (Appendix 9). Titles were also approved for units of the CEF in Canada. This included distinctive titles for each of the draft giving depot battalions formed during 1917. These were detailed in CEF Routine Orders (Canada) 492 and 541, 1918. (These Routine Orders are reproduced in Appendix 14.)

The following outlines the use and approval of shoulder titles in each component of the CEF.

Infantry

For infantry battalions in Canada and the UK the numeral was worn over INF which was worn over CANADA on the shoulder straps. e.g.:[11]

14
INF
CANADA

The above were three separate pieces, but in a few cases the battalion had the three pieces brazed together. Photographs show that some of the battalions wore the numeral and CANADA only.

A number of battalions introduced their own titles. Some wore the battalion numeral over CANADA (one piece), and some added the crown, a beaver or their sub-title; others were fancier designs on a solid plate. Some battalions (other than those of the 1st Contingent) wore cloth shoulder titles.[12] Only a few of these were approved.

In France the Royal Canadian Regiment, Princess Patricia's Canadian Light Infantry, 5th, 13th, 14th, 16th, 24th, 42nd Battalions wore their own titles. The rest of the infantry battalions wore only the CANADA title.[10] Members of the machine gun section of the infantry battalions also wore MGS on the shoulder straps. Although contrary to regulations, it is known that at times the C over numeral collar badge was worn on the shoulder straps over the CANADA title.[13]

Figure 51 *Examples of separate titles brazed together (reduced)*
Author's collection

Figure 52 *Cpl J. H. McQuarrie, 105th Battalion of PEI wearing cloth shoulder flash*
Prince Edward Island Regiment Military Museum

Artillery

The field batteries in Canada were approved to use the battery numeral and C.F.A on their shoulder straps along with the CANADA title.[14] Some batteries wore the numeral and C.F.A as two pieces. Others had them made into one piece - some with the battery numeral and C.F.A in one line, some in two lines. The 64th, 65th, 76th and 79th Depot Batteries had titles with the battery numeral over C.F.A over CANADA. This was approved for the 64th and 79th Batteries, but a request for approval by the 65th Battery was denied. They used the title anyway.

Figure 53 *Examples of styles of Field Battery titles (reduced)*

Author's collection

The 1st Battery CFA had the title 1st over C.F.A over CANADA and the 50th Depot Battery the title Q over 50 C.F.A. A request by the 50th Battery for a distinctive title had been denied. An unusual title for the 78th Depot Battery recently appeared in an auction.[15] It consists of the gun wheel containing 78 over CANADA in one piece. None of these titles were approved. Siege batteries in Canada likely wore the battery numeral and C.G.A with the CANADA title. Some of the heavy artillery units had distinctive titles as follows:

Figure 54 *A soldier wearing the cloth shoulder flash of the 207th Battalion*

Charles Hamilton collection

PEI Heavy Brigade Draft	P.E.I.H.B[16]
No 6 Battery Siege Artillery	See Figure 55
McGill Overseas Siege Artillery Draft	See Figure 56
King's County PEI Siege Artillery Draft	distinctive design[c1]
No 5 PEI Siege Artillery Draft	See Figure 58

For the most part, the batteries in France wore only the CANADA title and C.F.A or C.G.A. However, the 11th Siege Battery reported in February 1918 that other ranks were wearing 11 over C.G.A. over CANADA, three separate pieces.[17] For the Ammunition Columns unapproved metal titles were made reading D.A.C, 2 over D.A.C and B.A.C. It is not known if these were worn in France.

Figure 55 Shoulder Title, No 6 Battery Siege Artillery

John Swan collection

Figure 56 Shoulder Title, McGill Overseas Siege Artillery Draft

John Swan collection

Figure 57 A few distinctive Infantry Battalion titles (reduced) 104th Bn title, John Swan collection

Other titles Author's collection

Figure 58 *Shoulder Title, No 5 PEI Siege Artillery Draft (enlarged)*

Greg Gallant collection

Figure 59 *3rd Divisional Cavalry Squadron title*

Douglas E Light collection

Cavalry and Mounted Rifles

Most of the Cavalry units wore distinctive shoulder titles as follows:

Canadian Cavalry Brigade	
The Royal Canadian Dragoons	R.C.D
Lord Strathcona's Horse	L.S.H
(Royal Canadians)	STRATHCONA'S
The Fort Garry Horse	FORT-GARRY over HORSE
	(cloth, yellow on black)
	F.G.H
	FGH over CANADA
Canadian Light Horse	C.L.H
Royal North West Mounted Police Squadron	RNWMP
Special Service Squadron,	
19th Alberta Dragoons	Description unknown[18]
3rd Divisional Cavalry Squadron	Figure 59

The Royal Canadian Dragoons and the Lord Strathcona's Horse, being permanent force units were issued with titles from Ordnance Stores from the beginning of the war. The Fort Garry Horse and Canadian Light Horse titles (but not those of the Royal North West Mounted Police Squadron) were provided by the Canadian Ordnance Depot after the fall of 1917.

The Canadian mounted rifles regiments wore a variety of titles as follows:

1st CMR	distinctive design in matched pairs[c2]
2nd CMR	distinctive design[c3]
	cloth, BRITISH COLUMBIA over 2 over CMR,
	(yellow on khaki)
3rd CMR	cloth, 3 over C M R, white on khaki
4th CMR	4 over C.M.R (two pieces)
5th CMR	See Figure 60
8th CMR	8 over C.M.R[c4]

Figure 60 *Shoulder title worn by the 5th Canadian Mounted Rifles Battalion*

Charles Hamilton collection

9th CMR	distinctive design[c5]
10th CMR	distinctive design[c6]
11th CMR	distinctive design[c7]
12th CMR	12 over C.M.R over CANADA (one piece)
	12 over CANADA plate (two pieces)[19]
13th CMR	13 over C.M.R[c8]
	13 over M.R over CANADA plate (three pieces)[20]

Only the 9th CMR title was approved. Titles reading C.M.R over CANADA and M.R were also used. The Canadian Mounted Rifles Remount Depot wore the title REMOUNTS.

Engineers and Pioneers

Initially the Canadian Engineers wore the metal title C.E which was issued by Ordnance Stores.[21] Field Companies wore the numeral over the title. These were replaced in the field for all the Engineer units with a worsted title C E in blue letters on a red patch.[22] These were worn on the divisional formation patch, where these existed. The Tunnelling Companies used the title T.C [23] which had not been approved. The engineer and pioneer units used the following titles:

Canadian Engineers	CE
	CE (cloth, blue on red)
Engineer Training Depot	CE
	SIGNAL
1st Pioneer Battalion	distinctive design[c9]; PIONEERS[c9]
2nd Pioneer Battalion	cloth, 2 over CANADIAN over
	PIONEERS, (cloth, yellow on black)
3rd Pioneer Battalion	PIONEERS
4th Pioneer Battalion	4CP; PIONEERS
5th Pioneer Battalion	cloth, 5 over PIONEERS over
	CANADA (bronze on khaki) (figure 61)
Pioneer Draft	distinctive design[c10]
Pioneer Training Depot	PIONEERS

Only the titles worn by the Engineer units, the Engineer Training Depot and the 5th Pioneer Battalion were approved.

A cloth title reading WINNIPEG in blue letters on khaki has been seen on a uniform bearing the distinguishing patch of the 1st Divisional Engineers.[24]

Figure 61 A sapper in the 5th Pioneer Battalion wearing their cloth shoulder title

Charles Hamilton collection

Labour Group

The 4th Canadian Labour Battalion had a distinctive shoulder title[c11] which had not been approved. The 1st, 2nd and 3rd Canadian Labour Battalions, 1st to 4th Entrenching Battalions, 1st to 4th Infantry Works Companies simply wore the CANADA title.

Machine Gun Corps

Brigade Machine Gun Companies wore the numeral over M.G.C over CANADA, in three separate pieces.[25] Later many of the machine gun units wore only the CANADA shoulder title. Some units may have worn an unapproved C.M.G.C title as well. A few distinctive titles are known:

Automobile Machine Gun Brigade No 1	See Figure 62
Eaton Motor Machine Gun Battery	distinctive design[c12]
Yukon Motor Machine Gun Battery	distinctive design[26]
Canadian Machine Gun Depot	Officers[c13, 27]
	Other Ranks*[c14, 27]
	*also worn in France[28]
3rd Machine Gun Company	See Figure 63
86th Machine Gun Battalion	86MG
New Brunswick Machine Gun Draft	See Figure 64

The only title approved by militia headquarters was that for the 86th Machine Gun Battalion. The British cloth title MOTOR MACHINE over GUNS, red letters on khaki, appear to have been worn by Canadian Units occasionally.[30]

Figure 62 Shoulder title, Automobile Machine Gun Brigade No 1

Ron Edwards collection

Figure 63 Shoulder title, 3rd Machine Gun Company[29]

Ron Edwards collection

Service Corps

The Canadian Army Service Corps CEF had two titles, an unapproved distinctive title[c15] and the title C.A.S.C. The latter was approved 30 April 1915[31] and was worn above the title CANADA. Also approved in the Dress Regulations was the title M.T for the Mechanical Transport Services of the Corps. Some of the Service Corps units had distinctive titles:

No 8 "Overseas" Depot Unit of Supply	8 over A.S.C. (on a plate)
	8 A.S.C
19th Company CASC	19 over C.A.S.C
4th Divisional Train	distinctive design[c16]
Mechanical Transport Company	distinctive design[c17]
	M.T
Divisional Ammunition Park	D.A.P
1st Divisional Ammunition Park	1 over D.A.P over CANADA
Divisional Supply Column	See Figure 65
1st Overseas Training Depot C.A.S.C.	distinctive design[c18]

None of the above titles was approved.

Figure 64 *Shoulder title, New Brunswick Machine Gun Draft*

Author's collection

Figure 65 *Shoulder title Divisional Supply Column*

Author's collection

Medical Services

The unit numeral over the title AMB over the CANADA title (three separate pieces) were worn initially by units of the 1st Contingent and the 2nd Division.[2,3] On 30 April 1915 the title C.A.M.C was approved[31] and was worn over the CANADA title. Some of the medical units had distinctive titles:

No 1 Field Ambulance	distinctive design[c19]
No 2 Field Ambulance	2 F over A M B (makeshift title)
	No 2 FIELD AMBULANCE (red on khaki)[32]
No 3 Field Ambulance	distinctive design[c20]
No 4 Field Ambulance	distinctive design[c21]
No 8 Field Ambulance	distinctive design[c22]
No 9 Field Ambulance	distinctive design[c23]
	9th FLD.AMB over CANADA, (blue on khaki)
No 10 Field Ambulance	distinctive design[c24]
No 1 Casualty Clearing Station	1 over CCS over CANADA[33]
No 2 Casualty Clearing Station	2 over CCS over CANADA[c25]

No 6 Stationary Hospital	LAVAL worn with C.A.M.C
(later No 6 General Hospital)	and CANADA
(Laval University)	[titles in three separate pieces)

Only No 6 Stationary Hospital's title was approved. No 9 Field Ambulance claimed their title was approved February 1916 and No 10 Field Ambulance stated their title had been approved by ADMS MD No 10, but nothing was located in Militia Headquarters files for either of these units.

Forestry Corps

The Canadian Forestry Corps did not have a special title for use by their depots, companies and drafts. They probably only used the CANADA title. Two of the forestry battalions wore distinctive shoulder titles:

| 224th Forestry Battalion | 224 over CANADA |
| 230th Forestry Battalion | 230 over CANADA |

Only the title for the 230th Battalion was approved.

Railway Troops

The following titles are known to have been used:

Canadian Railway Construction Corps	CONSTR
No 1 Construction Battalion	CONSTR
No 2 Construction Battalion	distinctive design[c26]
218th Railway Construction Battalion	See Figure 66
228th Railway Construction Battalion	See Figure 67
239th Railway Construction Battalion	239 over CANADA
	(different styles for Officers and ORs)
256th "Overseas" Railway	
Construction Battalion	256RY over CANADA
Corps of Canadian Railway Troops	C.R.T
Canadian Railway Troops Depot	RAILWAY, C.R.T.
Skilled Railway Employees	S.R.E over CANADA

Figure 66 Shoulder title, 218th Railway Construction Battalion

Author's collection

Figure 67 Shoulder title, 228th Railway Construction Battalion

Author's collection

Only the titles for No 1 Construction Battalion, 228th Construction Battalion and the Corps of Canadian Railway Troops were officially approved.

Canadian Garrison Regiment

There were battalions in each MD and separate titles are known reading 1BN, 2BN, 3BN, 4BN, 5BN, 6BN, 11BN, 12BN, 13BN and also the title C.G.R. These titles were approved.[34] The titles 7BN and 10BN have not yet been seen. There also was an unapproved 5th Battalion title 5 over C.G.R.

Other Corps and Services, Miscellaneous Units

Shoulder titles were in use by the following units:

Canadian Signal Service	SIGNAL
	CANADIAN over
	SIGNAL CORPS
Canadian Army Dental Corps	C.A.D.C
Canadian Ordnance Corps	C.O.C
No 4 Detachment	See Figure 68
Canadian Army Pay Corps	C.A.P.C
Canadian Army Veterinary Corps	C.A.V.C
Canadian Postal Corps	C.P.C
Canadian Chaplain Service	no special title
Military Police	no special title
Canadian Military Police Corps	no special title
No 1 Detachment, London, Ont	See Figure 69
Canadian Corps Cyclists	CYCLIST
	CYCLISTS over CANADA
1st Divisional Cyclist Company	CYCLISTS
3rd Divisional Cyclist Company	3 over CYCLISTS
Reserve Cyclist Company	CYCLISTS
Canadian Tank Corps	T.C
Canadian Army Gymnastic Staff	C.A.G.S
Corps of Military Staff Clerks	C.M.S.C
Headquarters Staff	H.Q.S
	H.Q.S over CANADA
Depot Battalions	see Appendix 14
Syren Party (part of the Special Mobile	
Force, Murmansk, code name "Syren")	See Figure 70
British Columbia Reinforcements	B.C. over CANADA (on a plate)
Y.M.C.A. Military Services	Y.M.C.A
	Y.M.C.A (on a plate)

Of the above titles, SIGNAL, C.A.D.C, C.A.V.C, T.C, C.A.G.S, C.M.S.C, CYCLISTS were known to have been approved officially.

Figure 68 No 4 Detachment Canadian Ordnance Corps

John Swan collection

Figure 69 No 1 Detachment Canadian Military Police Corps

Author's collection

Figure 70 Syren Party (Murmansk) [35]

Author's collection

References - Cross' catalogue numbers

c1. 150-3-7	c7. 10-7-11	c14. 45-1-3 top title	c21. 85-7-4
c2. 10-7-1	c8. 10-7-13	c15. 95-1-1	c22. 85-7-8
c3. 10-7-2	c9. 70-3-1	c16. 95-7-4	c23. 85-7-9
c4. 10-7-8	c10. 70-3-3	c17. 95-9-1	c24. 85-7-10
c5. 10-7-9	c11. 70-9-4	c18. 95-17-1	c25. 85-5-2
c6. 10-7-10	c12. 50-3-3	c19. 85-7-1	c26. 65-3-2
	c13. 45-1-3 bottom title	c20. 85-7-3	

Chapter 8

Odds and Ends

Pipe Band Badges

Stewart identified fifty-four CEF units that had pipe bands. Those pipe bands that wore special badges on their glengarry (or cap in one instance) were:

Princess Patricia's Canadian Light Infantry	Figure 71
19th Battalion	distinctive badge in white metal[1]
26th Battalion	distinctive badge in white metal[2]
29th Battalion	Clan MacKinnon badge[c1]
102nd Battalion	distinctive badge[c2]
107th Battalion	distinctive badge[3, c3]
173rd Battalion	Figure 72
Canadian Forestry Corps	distinctive badge in white metal[4]

None of these badges was approved officially. There also is a badge[c4] which has been thought of as that of the 49th Battalion Pipe Band. Recent research into this badge casts doubt that it is from the World War I period, and is more likely of the militia of the early 1920s.[5]

The pipers of the 21st Battalion pipe band initially wore the battalion badge in brass on the glengarry. Beginning in 1917 the battalion badge with a brass CANADA shoulder title (curved upwards) underneath were mounted on a piece of metal and attached to a square piece of Argyll and Sutherland Highlanders tartan.[6] The 29th Battalion pipe band was presented with the Clan MacKinnon banner by the 35th Chief of the Clan at Shorncliffe at an unknown date in 1915. After presenting the banner, the Hon Mrs MacKinnon of MacKinnon gave each piper the clan crest in hand-cut sterling. This became

Figure 71 *Replica of PPCLI Pipe Band Badge*
Author's collection

Figure 72 *173rd Battalion Pipe Band Badge*
Bob Russell collection

the band's badge.[7] The 67th, 113th, 134th and 224th Battalion pipe bands wore the battalion badge in white metal[4] and the pipers of the 228th, 231st and 241st Battalions wore the battalion badge in silver[8] on the glengarry. The pipers of the 228th Battalion also wore the battalion grenade collar badge[c5] in silver.[8] The drummers of the 96th Battalion pipe band appear to wear the battalion badges in white metal.[9] There is a civil-

Figure 73   A soldier of the 236th Battalion Maclean Highlanders. The enlargement shows the Battalion badge on the sporran
        Elbow War Museum collection

ian band in Saskatoon known as the 96th Battalion Canadian Highlanders Pipe Band. They wear a restrike of the 96th Battalion glengarry badge in a dull brown finish.

Stewart also indicated that forty-six of the pipe bands wore the kilt. A number of these wore a variety of badges on the sporran which are listed in Appendix 15. In three instances badges were placed on the waistbelt buckle. The 25th Battalion had both the battalion badge and the Seaforth Highlanders badge in silver on the shoulder belt plate and the waistbelt buckle.[10] The 173rd and 231st Battalions placed the battalion badge in silver on their buckles.[11]

Highland Battalion Sporran Badges

There were twenty-eight highland battalions in the CEF, but only twenty-one wore the kilt and two of these did not wear the sporran. The officer's and other ranks in most of these battalions are known to have worn a badge on the sporran as follows:

13th Battalion (Royal Highlanders of Canada)	Sporran badge, The Black Watch (Royal Highland Regiment)[12]
15th Battalion (48th Highlanders of Canada)	Sporran badge, 48th Regiment 'Highlanders'[13]
16th Battalion (The Canadian Scottish)	Battalion cap badge[14]
43rd, 174th, 179th Battalions (Cameron Highlanders of Canada)	Sporran badge, The 79th Highlanders of Canada (Officers only for 174th and 179th Bns)[15]

72nd, 231st Battalions	Sporran badge, The 72nd Regiment
(Seaforth Highlanders of Canada)	Seaforth Highlanders of Canada[16]
85th, 185th, 193rd, 219th Battalions	Battalion cap badge[17]
(Nova Scotia Highlanders)	
92nd, 134th Battalions	Battalion cap badge[18]
(48th Highlanders of Canada)	
173rd Battalion	Battalion cap badge[19]
(Canadian Highlanders)	
236th Battalion	Battalion cap badge
(Maclean Highlanders)	

A picture of Lieutenant-Colonel Percy A Guthrie, OC of the battalion shows him wearing the badge of the Clan MacLean on the sporran (figure 74). It seems that the Officer Commanding wore this badge rather than the Battalion badge.

The 42nd and 73rd Battalions (Royal Highlanders of Canada) had the numeral 42 and 73 respectively on the flap of the sporran.[20] It is not known if the 241st Battalion (Canadian Scottish Borderers) wore a badge on the sporran.

Makeshift Battalion Badges

Cross catalogues some twenty makeshift battalion badges, mostly cap badges. Also a few hitherto unknown makeshift badges are in collections or have appeared recently in auctions.[21] These badges comprise the battalion number mounted on a General Service maple leaf. Some of these probably were temporary issues to the battalion while they were wait-

Figure 74 Lieutenant-Colonel Percy A Guthrie, OC 236th Battalion MacLean Highlanders. The enlargement shows the Clan MacLean badge on the sporran

Author's collection

ing for their supply of new badges or perhaps as an interim measure when the supply of badges was depleted. Possibly in some cases soldiers created a badge to replace one they lost or gave away. There also is the danger that some over enthusiastic collector made up the badge! It is impossible to authenticate most of these makeshift badges. The Will Bird collection contained the makeshift badges for the 2nd, 90th, 99th, 136th, 142nd and 168th Battalions[c6], and the Durand collection the makeshift badge of the 1st Battalion.[c7] One can be fairly confident of the authenticity of these badges at least.

***Figure 75** Some Makeshift Infantry Battalion Badges*[22]

Oddities and Unusual Battalion Badges

During the author's research in the CEF records at the National Archives a few instances were noted where a unit submitted a sample badge for approval rather than a drawing. It became obvious that sometimes a manufacturer produced prototypes of badges in an attempt to obtain the order. A number of unusual battalion badges[23] have been catalogued by Cross and likely these were samples or prototypes. Regarding the unusual 3rd Battalion cap badge[c8] Clawson's Notes stated:

> Lieutenant-Colonel Allan late of the 3rd Battalion and one of a committee chosen to prepare a design for a regimental badge, says he never saw such a badge as this and doubts if it was ever used.

Two manufacturers in the UK appear to have produced custom-made battalion cap badges. Tiptafts of Birmingham produced a cap badge for the 9th Battalion[c9] and the 10th Battalion.[c10] Reiche of Folkestone produced a similar design of badges for the 9th, 19th and 20th Battalions.[c11] The Glenbow Museum collection has a cap badge of the 73rd Battalion which appear to be custom-made.[24] Unusual cap badges for No 1 Construction Battalion and 1st Canadian Motor Machine Gun Brigade were offered in a recent militaria

***Figure 76** Unusual cap badges of the 105th and 169th Battalions*

Figure 77 Unusual cap badges of the 88th, 147th, 101st and 168th Battalions[27] (slightly reduced)

auction. These appear to be custom-made officer's badges.[25]

There is another group of three unusual battalion badges. Each comprises an eight-pointed diamond cut star with the battalion collar badge mounted thereon. They are for the 105th, 151st[c12] and 169th Battalions. It is unknown where and by whom these were worn and if they are in fact authentic items.

The first issue of the 151st Battalion badges[c13] contained the wording "Central Alberta Battalion". This was an error by the maker Jackson Bros, Edmonton. Approval for this badge was requested from militia headquarters but the request was denied. Consequently Jackson Bros were required to re-make the badges with the approved wording "Central Alberta Canada". There is an unusual cap badge known for the 147th Battalion. Sgt Thomas Bradley[26] an original member of the 147th Battalion, told the Author he had never seen this badge.

Eaton's Pattern Battalion Items

Cross catalogues as "cap badges" some thirty-nine infantry battalion items made by Caron Bros for the T Eaton Company. These are all of similar design with a different battalion number. They are also known for the 154th and 198th Battalions (not listed in Cross). It is known that seventeen of these badges had original pin fasteners and four had new lugs soldered on them. The Author has the 85th Battalion item with original lugs. It is interesting to note that of the forty different items known, exactly half were for battalions raised in Toronto and vicinity. The following appeared in the daily T Eaton Company advertisement published in the 3 May 1916 issue of *The Toronto Daily News*:

MILITARY BADGES AND BROOCHES, SOLDIERS' NEEDS, ETC.,
DISPLAYED AT THE CENTRE STAIRWAY, MAIN FLOOR

Large Maple Leaf brooch, with local battalion numbers as worn by overseas troops, such as 74th, 75th, 83rd, 204th, etc. Obtainable in gilt or antique bronze finish. Each...25¢

It appears that these so-called Eaton's pattern "badges" are in fact sweetheart pins or brooches. Given that the author's specimen of the 85th Battalion has its original lugs it is possible that some may have been used as cap badges.

Makeshift Artillery Cap Badges

In chapter 3, under Field Artillery, reference was made to the existence of general issue Canada artillery gun cap badges with the numerals 1 to 9 and letters A to E, H and T mounted on the wheel. All but those with the letters E, H and T are illustrated in Cross as "Training Batteries".[28] Those with the letters E, H and T were illustrated in auction catalogues.[29] The Author has not been able to verify with any certainty that these are CEF badges. The following information is provided:

***Figure 78** Eaton's pattern item for 154th Battalion*

Bob Russell collection

(a) These badges have appeared in auctions since 1990. None of these were in the Durand or Will Bird collections, nor were they mentioned in Duncan's notes on CEF badges. However those with 1, 3, 4, 5, 6, 7, 8, 9, A, D thereon are found in the Canadian War Museum CEF collection.

(b) No references were found to Training Batteries in the CEF records in the National Archives of Canada. Training was conducted in the original CFA Battery, Artillery Draft or the 44th to 78th Depot Batteries.

(c) There were Nos 1 to 7, 10 to 13 Artillery Depots, CEF authorized in Canada on 27 September 1918. (CEF (Canada) Routine Order 1123)

(d) A Table showing all Artillery Formations and Batteries in the CEF prepared by the Army Historical Section, shows the Batteries formed in Canada and overseas:

> 1st, 2nd, 3rd Depot Batteries CFA formed 19 December 1914 at Salisbury Plain; redesignated 1st, 2nd, 3rd Batteries Reserve Brigade CFA; absorbed on reorganization by the Canadian Reserve Artillery (CRA) 12 June 1917.
>
> 1st, 2nd, 3rd, 4th, 5th Batteries CRA formed 7 November 1916 at Shorncliffe; redesignated A, B, C, D, E Batteries CRA, 12 June 1917.
>
> E Battery Anti-Aircraft - formed January 1917 in France
>
> C Overseas Casualty Battery - formed in the United Kingdom
>
> *Note*: There never were any 6th, 7th, 8th, 9th Reserve Depot Batteries or H or T Batteries formed.

(e) It is possible some of these makeshift cap badges were used by the above depots or batteries, but that is pure speculation. The Canadian Reserve Artillery at Witley reported 13 November 1917 that they used the "Universal Artillery cap badge precisely the same as Imperial cap badge with Canada where Ubique is".[30]

Variations in Dies

The first issue of badges for most of the units raised after the 1st Contingent were made in Canada. After their arrival in the UK, makers there often made CEF badges using their own dies. A comparison of these different dies reveals differences such as:

- shape of the maple leaf
- style of the numerals
- size of the beaver
- plain versus framed ribbons or tablets
- periods versus no periods in motto
- size and shape of crown
- number of jewels in the crown

A large number of the UK issues are found in a brown service dress finish compared with the pickled finish used by most Canadian makers.

Cap Badges at the Canadian Corps Reunion

A reunion of the Canadian Corps took place in Toronto during 1934. Many CEF cap badges were restruck and sold at the reunion. These restrikes were in yellow brass for the most part, not the pickled, browning, black or antique finish of the original CEF badges.[31]

References - Cross' catalogue numbers

c1.	29C	c7.	1D
c2.	102C	c8.	3A
c3.	107C	c9.	9A
c4.	49C	c10.	10B
c5.	228	c11.	9A
c6.	2D		19C
	90B		20C
	99B	c12.	151C
	136B	c13.	151B
	142B		
	168C		

Epilogue

Reorganization and Perpetuation

The Canadian Militia was reorganized during 1920-21. It was decided to provide a permanent link between the CEF units and the militia units. A scheme was introduced whereby the cavalry, artillery, infantry and machine gun units of the militia were granted "perpetuation" of the CEF mounted rifle regiments, artillery brigades and batteries, infantry battalions and machine gun units. Perpetuation was granted for the most part on either the recruiting of, or contributions by, the militia unit for a CEF unit, or the fact that the CEF unit was raised in the area of the militia unit. In some cases perpetuation was granted arbitrarily. Most reorganized militia units received new or altered designations. The numerals in the title were removed from a few of the cavalry regiments and all but one of the infantry regiments.

Regarding badges for the reorganized units, MO 204, 13 April 1921 was issued stating:

> Maple Leaf Cap and Collar badges are available in Ordnance Stores and may be issued in the usual manner to all units of the Non-Permanent Active Militia, as a temporary measure, until such time as Badges and Crests, which have been submitted to Militia Headquarters, have been approved of and issued.

Three regiments immediately issued new badges which reflected their perpetuation of CEF battalions:

	Included in the badge design:
The Manitoba Rangers	'45' for 45th Battalion[a1]
The Edmonton Fusiliers	"9th CEF" for 9th Battalion[a2]
The Colchester and Hants Regiment	"25' for 25th Battalion[a3]

These badges were never approved and were rendered incorrect under Militia Headquarters Circular Letters in 1921:

> . . . it will not be permissible for a number or numeral to be borne on a regimental crest or cap badge, except in such cases where a number is part of the title of the regiment as a whole.[1]

There was no objections in the circular letters to the collar badges of militia regiments' referring to their perpetuated CEF battalion. These militia units included such a reference on their new collar badges:

	Included in the collar badge design:
The Eastern Townships Mounted Rifles	'5' for 5th CMR Battalion[a4]
1st Regiment The Alberta Mounted Rifles	'3 MR' for 3rd Regiment CMR[a5]
The Stormont and Glengarry Regiment	'154' for 154th Battalion[a6]
The Saint John Fusiliers	'CEF', '26', 'BATTALION' for the 26th Battalion[a7]
The Calgary Highlanders	'10th Canadians' for the 10th Battalion (not in Mazeas)
The Winnipeg Light Infantry	'10th CEF' for the 10th Battalion[a8]
The Vancouver Regiment	'29th Bn CEF' for 29th Battalion[a9]

| The Alberta Regiment | 'XXXI' for the 31st Battalion[a10] |
| The Toronto Scottish Regiment | '75' for the 75th Battalion[a11] |

Use of CEF Badges by Post War Units

After the war the Princess Patricia's Canadian Light Infantry and the 22nd (French Canadian) Battalion were reconstituted as permanent force units. During the reorganization of the militia the Officers and men of some of the CEF battalions that had served in France and Flanders with the Canadian Corps asked the militia authorities to reconstitute their battalion in the militia. This was done in some instances by authorizing a new regiment, or by using the establishment of an existing regiment. This in substance brought the battalion into the post-war militia. Officially these units were shown as perpetuating the battalion, but in fact the units considered themselves as a reconstitution of the CEF battalion.[2] In spite of the provisions of MO 204 these "reconstituted" units and some other militia units initially used the badges of their perpetuated CEF battalion:

Princess Patricia's Canadian Canadian Light Infantry	CEF unit badges[c1]
22nd Regiment	22nd Battalion badges[c2]
The Ottawa Highlanders	38th Battalion badges[c3]
The Cape Breton Highlanders	85th Battalion badges[c31]
The Prince Edward Island Regiment	105th Battalion badges[c4]
1st Battalion 1st British Columbia Regiment (Duke of Connaught's Own)	7th Battalion cap badge[c5] Offs, 7th Battalion collar badges[c5] ORs, C over 7 collar badges [3]
The North British Columbia Regiment	102nd Battalion badges without "Overseas' thereon[c6]
1st Battalion The Calgary Regiment (later The Calgary Highlanders)	10th Battalion badges[c7] 10th Battalion cap badge[c7] in white metal worn on the sporran
2nd Battalion The Calgary Regiment (later The Calgary Regiment)	50th Battalion badges[c8]
The Canadian Scottish Regiment	16th Battalion badges[c9]
The Royal Montreal Regiment	14th Battalion badges[4,c10]
The Toronto Regiment	3rd Battalion cap badge[5,c11] C over 3 collar badges
The Edmonton Regiment	49th Battalion badges[c12]
2nd Battalion The British Columbia Regiment (later The Vancouver Regiment)	29th Battalion badges[6, c13]
The West Toronto Regiment (amalgamated 1925)	20th Battalion cap badge[c14] General Service maple leaf collar badges[7]

The North British Columbia Regiment and The Toronto Regiment continued to wear these badges until 1936.[8] Neither received approval in general orders. The 14th Battalion badge was approved in general orders as the badge of The Royal Montreal Regiment.[4] All the other units received new badges approved between 1922-31. The Canadian Scottish Regiment, The Calgary Regiment and The Edmonton Regiment continued to wear the CEF design collar badges.

The Toronto Scottish Regiment probably wore the badges of the 75th Battalion until they received their badges approved in 1923. The Kootenay Regiment never had a new badge approved after 1920. Some members of the regiment were seen wearing the 54th Battalion badges.[9]

The 8th Battalion CEF adopted as its badge the design of its parent militia regiment with the scroll bearing the title "90th Winnipeg Rifles" removed. The badge was made in browning, black finish or sterling silver. The badge approved for The Winnipeg Rifles after the war (Mazeas M28) was identical in design to the 8th Battalion[c15] badge, but was in oxidized silver and black finish for Officers and black finish for Other Ranks.

The 1921 circular letters also stated:

> In the case of a regiment of cavalry or mounted rifles, or a battalion of infantry, the collar badge may be that of the CEF or Militia unit which it perpetuates.

These units wore CEF badges for collar badges:

The Canadian Scottish Regiment	16th Battalion design of officers collar badges worn by all ranks
The Regina Rifles	28th Battalion cap badge without 'Overseas'[c16] worn as collar badges
The Westminster Regiment	47th Battalion collar badges[c17] with motto added
The Calgary Regiment	50th Battalion collar badges[c8]
The South Alberta Regiment	31st Battalion collar badges[c18]
The Edmonton Regiment	49th Battalion collar badges[c12]
1st Motor Machine Gun Brigade	1st Canadian Motor Machine Gun Brigade collar badges[c19]

The CEF collar badge designs for all but The Calgary Regiment were approved in general orders during 1928-31.

Designs of Militia Regiment Badges based on CEF Badges

In several instances the design of the post war militia regiment's badges was based on those of their perpetuated CEF regiment or battalion:

The Saskatchewan Mounted Rifles	Badges[a12] based on 1st CMR Bn badges[c20]
The British Columbia Mounted Rifles	Badges[a13] based on 2nd CMR Bn badges[c21]
The Ontario Mounted Rifles	Cap badge[a14] based on 4th CMR Bn cap badge[c22]
The Eastern Townships Mounted Rifles	Badges[a4] based on 5th CMR Bn badges[c23]
The King's Canadian Hussars	Collar badge[a15] based on 5th CMR Bn collars[c24]
The Bruce Regiment	Collar badge[a16] based on 160th Bn collar badge[c25]

The Simcoe Foresters	Badges[a17] based on 157th and 177th Bn badges[c26]
The Winnipeg Light Infantry	Badges[a8] based on 10th Bn badges[c7]
The Cape Breton Highlanders	Badges[a18] based on 85th and 185th Bns Badges[c27]
The Algonquin Regiment	Badges[a19] based on 159th Bn badges[c28]
The Chasseurs Canadiens	Cap badge[a20] based on 167th Bn badges[c29]
The Kenora Light Infantry	Badges[a21] based on 94th Bn badges[c30]

References - Mazeas' and Cross' catalogue numbers

Mazeas

a1. M.147a	a12. C.34
a2. M.150	a13. C.44
a3. M.114	a14. C.18
a4. C.38	a15. C.25
a5. C.33	a16. M.55
a6. M.91	a17. M.58
a7. M.95	a18. M.137a
a8. M.159	a19. M.145
a9. M.22	a20. M.159
a10. M.164	a21. C.146
a11. M.166	

Cross

c1. Infantry p.2	c13. 29A	c23. 10-7-5
c2. 22B	c14. 20B	c24. 10-7-6
c3. 38	c15. 8A	c25. 160
c4. 105	c16. 28B	c26. 157A
c5. 7A	c17. 47 Jacoby #2	177A
c6. 102B	c18. 31A	c27. 185A
c7. 10A	c19. 50-1-1	c28. 159
c8. 50B	c20. 10-7-1	c29. 167
c9. 16	c21. 10-7-2A	c30. 94
c10. 14	10-7-2B	c31. 85a
c11. 3B	c22. 10-7-4A	
c12. 49B	10-7-4B	

Appendix 1
Abbreviations

A/	Acting
AAA	Acting Assistant Adjutant
AAG	Assistant Adjutant General
ADOS	Assistant Director Ordnance Services
AG	Adjutant General
BEF	British Expeditionary Force
CAMC	Canadian Army Medical Corps
CEF	Canadian Expeditionary Force
CFA	Canadian Field Artillery
CFC	Canadian Forestry Corps
CGA	Canadian Garrison Artillery
CGR	Canadian Garrison Regiment
CGS	Chief of the General Staff
CLH	Canadian Light Horse
CMGC	Canadian Machine Gun Corps
CMR	Canadian Mounted Rifles
COC	Canadian Ordnance Corps
COO	Chief Ordnance Officer
CRA	Canadian Reserve Artillery
CRO	Headquarters Canadians Routine Orders
CRT	Canadian Railway Troops
CTD	Canadian Training Division
DA	Deputy Adjutant
DAA	Deputy Assistant Adjutant
DAAG	Deputy Assistant Adjutant General
DCO	Deputy Commanding Officer
DEOS	Director of Equipment and Ordnance Services
DHH	Director History and Heritage
D of A	Director of Artillery
DOC	District Officer Commanding
DOS	Director Ordnance Services
GHQ	General Headquarters
GO	General Order
GOC	General Officer Commanding
GRO	General Routine Order
HQ	Headquarters

MD	Military District
MGC	Machine Gun Corps (British)
MO	Militia Order
OC	Officer Commanding
OMFC	Overseas Military Forces of Canada
QMG	Quartermaster General
RCHA	Royal Canadian Horse Artillery
RO	Routine Order
RNWMP	Royal North West Mounted Police
SSO	Senior Staff Officer
UK	United Kingdom

Appendix 2

Approval of Badges

Unit	Type[1]	Design[2]	Approval[3]
1st Canadian Division **1st Infantry Brigade**			
1st Battalion	cap col	1A C/1	) 1 Aug 18, GRO 4663)
2nd Battalion	cap col	2C C/2	) 1 Aug 18, GRO 4663)
3rd Battalion	cap col	3B C/3	) 1 Aug 18, GRO 4663)
4th Battalion	cap col	4B C/4	) 1 Aug 18, GRO 4663)
2nd Infantry Brigade			
5th Battalion	cap col	5A C/5	) 1 Aug 18, GRO 4663)
7th Battalion	cap col	7A C/7	) 1 Aug 18, GRO 4663)
8th Battalion	cap col	8A C/8	) 1 Aug 18, GRO 4663)
10th Battalion	cap col	10A C/10	) 1 Aug 18, GRO 4663) (approval of 10A originally requested 9 Nov 1915, Folder 6, File 2, Vol 3876*)
3rd Infantry Brigade			
13th Battalion	glen/bal col	hackle C/13	) 1 Aug 18, GRO 4663) (red hackle in lieu of badge)
14th Battalion	cap col	14 C/14	cited as 15 Oct 15, 683-136-2, Vol 1539, letter not on file 1 Aug 18, GRO 4663
15th Battalion	glen/bal col	15A C/15	) 1 Aug 18, GRO 4663)
16th Battalion	glen/bal col	16 C/16	) 1 Aug 18, GRO 4663, originally) approved by Gen Alderson, letter 31 May 1915, 4-2-18, Vol 8*

2nd Canadian Division
4th Infantry Brigade

18th Battalion	cap	18A	) 11 Aug 18, GRO 4663 (approval
	col	C/18	) of cap badge originally requested
			1 Aug 16, Folder 3, File 1, Vol
			4099*, no reply on file)
19th Battalion	cap	19A	) 11 Aug 18, GRO 4663 (approval
	col	C/19	) of cap badge originally requested
			1 Aug 16, Folder 3, File 1, Vol
			4099*, no reply on file)
20th Battalion	cap	20A	) 11 Aug 18, GRO 4663 (approval
	col	C/20	) of cap badge originally requested
			1 Aug 16, Folder 3, File 1, Vol
			4099*, no reply on file)
	off cap & col	20B	19 Dec 17, Folder 2, File 8,
			Q/23/4, Vol 4083*
21st Battalion	cap	21	) 11 Aug 18, GRO 4663 (approval
	col	C/21	) of cap badge originally requested
			1 Aug 16, Folder 3, File 1, Vol
			4099*, no reply on file)

5th Infantry Brigade

22nd Battalion	cap	22B	) 1 Aug 18, GRO 4663
	col	C/22	)
24th Battalion	cap	24	) 1 Aug 18, GRO 4663
	col	C/24	)
	Off col	VRC in script	(originally approved GO 29/1879)
25th Battalion	cap & col	25	) 18 May 15, 683-8-1, Vol 1509
	off col	25	)
	col	C/25	1 Aug 18, GRO 4663
26th Battalion	cap	26	) 1 Aug 18, GRO 4663
	col	C/26	)

6th Infantry Brigade

27th Battalion	cap	27	) 1 Aug 18, GRO 4663
	col	C/27	) (cap badge presented by Mayor of
			the City of Winnipeg, in Apr
			1915, Folder 54, File 13,
			Vol 4693*)
28th Battalion	cap	28A	) 1 Aug 18, GRO 4663
	col	C/28	)
29th Battalion	cap	29A	) 1 Aug 18, GRO 4663
	col	C/29	)

31st Battalion	cap col	31A C/31	) 1 Aug 18, GRO 4663)

3rd Canadian Division
7th Infantry Brigade

Royal Canadian Regiment	cap & col	page 3	21 Mar 16, 4-2-18, Vol 8* (cap badge originally approved GO 26/1911; collar badge by GO 35/1894) 1 Aug 18, GRO 4663
Princess Patricia's Canadian Light Infantry	cap & col	page 2	20 Mar 16, 4-2-18, Vol 8* 1 Aug 18, GRO 4663
42nd Battalion	glen/bal col	hackle C/42	) 1 Aug 18, GRO 4663) (red hackle in lieu of badge)
49th Battalion	cap col	49B C/49	) 1 Aug 18, GRO 4663)

8th Infantry Brigade

1st CMR Bn	cap & col[4]	10-7-1	1 Aug 18, GRO 4663
2nd CMR Bn	cap & col[4]	10-7-2A	1 Aug 18, GRO 4663
4th CMR Bn	cap&m/col[4]	10-7-4B	1 Aug 18, GRO 4663
5th CMR Bn	cap & col[4]	10-7-5	1 Aug 18, GRO 4663

9th Infantry Brigade

43rd Battalion	glen/bal col	43B C/43	) 1 Aug 18, GRO 4663)
52nd Battalion	cap col	52 C/52	) 1 Aug 18, GRO 4663)
58th Battalion	cap col	58B C/58	) 1 Aug 18, GRO 4663)
60th Battalion (replaced by the 116th Battalion)	cap & col	60	cited as 23 May 16, 683-95-6, Vol 1532, letter not on file
116th Battalion	cap & col col	116 C/116	18 Jan 16, 683-228-1, Vol 1546 1 Aug 18, GRO 4663

4th Canadian Division

10th Infantry Brigade

44th Battalion	cap	44A	) 1 Aug 18, GRO 4663
	col	C/44	)
46th Battalion	cap & col	46A	20 Oct 15, 683-56-1, Vol 1523
	col	C/46	1 Aug 18, GRO 4663
47th Battalion	cap	47#2	) 1 Aug 18, GRO 4663
	col	C/47	)
50th Battalion	cap & col	50A	18 May 15, 683-38-1, Vol 1519
	cap	50B	) 1 Aug 18, GRO 4663
	col	C/50	) (Approval of 50B originally requested 22 Jun 1917, B-4-3, Vol 884*, no reply on file)

11th Infantry Brigade

54th Battalion	cap & col	54	17 Aug 15, 683-68-5, Vol 1526
	col	C/54	1 Aug 18, GRO 4663
75th Battalion	cap	75A	) 1 Aug 18, GRO 4663
	col	C/75	)
87th Battalion	col	87-41/43	21 Nov 16, 683-132-1, Vol 1539
	col	C/87	1 Aug 18, GRO 4663
102nd Battalion	cap & col	102A	26 May 16, 683-274-1, Vol 1640
	col	C/102	1 Aug 18, GRO 4663

12th Infantry Brigade

38th Battalion	cap	38	) 1 Aug 18, GRO 4663
	collar	C/38	)
72nd Battalion	glen/bal	72	1 Aug 18, GRO 4663
	col	72	11 Sep 15, 683-103-4, Vol 1534
	col	C/72	1 Aug 18, GRO 4663 (Glengarry badge is of the parent militia which was not approved in GOs)
78th Battalion	cap	78	1 Aug 18, GRO 4663
	col	78	11 Aug 15, 683-113-1, Vol 1537
	col	C/78	1 Aug 18, GRO 4663
85th Battalion	bal & col	85A	18 Feb 16, 683-145-2, Vol 1540 (both styles of col)
	col	C/85	1 Aug 18, GRO 4663

Reinforcing Battalions

37th Battalion	cap & col	37A	12 July 15, 683-47-2, Vol 1521
40th Battalion	cap & col	40	15 July 15, 683-39-1, Vol 1519
51st Battalion	cap & col	51A	9 Dec 15, 683-21-1, Vol 1514
59th Battalion	cap & col	59C	11 Sep 15, 683-111-1, Vol 1536
68th Battalion	cap & col	68	25 Sep 15, 683-137-2, Vol 1539
69th Battalion	cap & col	69	1 Oct 15, 683-128-2, Vol 1539
74th Battalion	cap & col	74A	30 Aug 15, 683-120-1, Vol 1538
76th Battalion	cap & col	76	25 Sep 15, 683-135-1, Vol 1539
77th Battalion	cap & col	77	11 Sep 15, 683-79-2, Vol 1529
79th Battalion	cap & col	79	1 Oct 15, 683-140-2, Vol 1540
80th Battalion	cap & col	80	14 Oct 15, 683-108-4, Vol 1535
81st Battalion	cap & col cap & col	81A note	27 Nov 15) 683-163-1, Vol 1541 12 Apr 16) Note: Design with motto "vertus mille scuta" approved, but never made (figure 80)
83rd Battalion	cap & col	83A	14 Feb 16, 683-109-4, Vol 1535
86th Battalion - see Machine Gun			
89th Battalion	cap & col	89	27 Nov 15, 683-157-1, Vol 1541
90th Battalion	col	90A	27 Dec 15, 683-185-1, Vol 1543
91st Battalion	cap & col	91	28 Jun 16, 683-195-1, Vol 1544
92nd Battalion	bal & m/col	92B	20 Dec 15, 683-110-2, Vol 1536
95th Battalion	cap & col	95A	18 Nov 15, 683-158-1, Vol 1541
96th Battalion	cap & m/col	96	23 Mar 16, 683-224-3, Vol 1546
97th Battalion	cap & col	97B	15 Jan 16, 683-174-1, Vol 1542, approval withdrawn 26 April 16
	cap & col	97A	27 May 16, 683-174-1, Vol 1542
98th Battalion	cap & col	98	29 Jan 16, 683-179-2, Vol 1542
99th Battalion	cap & col	note	25 Feb 16, 683-260-1, Vol 1548 Note: Design approved different from 99A (figure 80), 47-3-12, Vol 4260
100th Battalion	cap	100	Badge of the parent militia regiment approved by GO 58/1913

Figures 79–80 Approved designs of 81st and 99th Battalions, different from those in use

NAC RG24

106th Battalion	cap & col	106	8 Apr 16, 683-256-1, Vol 1548
107th Battalion	cap & m/col	70-3-107	21 Dec 15, 683-183-1, Vol 1543
108th Battalion	cap & col	108B	14 Apr 16, 683-291-2, Vol 1650
109th Battalion	cap & col	109	cited as 22 Jan 16, 683-182-1, Vol 1543, letter not on file
112th Battalion	cap & col	112	8 Apr 16, 683-315-2, Vol 1661
113th Battalion	cap, bal & col	113	14 Feb 16, 683-172-2, Vol 1542
114th Battalion	cap & col	114	3 Mar 16, 683-173-1, Vol 1542
117th Battalion	cap & col	117	18 May 16, 683-265-2, Vol 1565
118th Battalion	cap & col	118A	30 Mar 16, 683-275-1, Vol 1642
119th Battalion	cap & col	119	17 May 16, 683-177-2, Vol 1542
120th Battalion	cap & col	120A	1 Mar 16, 683-272-1, Vol 1640
122nd Battalion also see Forestry	cap & col	122B	24 Jan 16, 683-236-1, Vol 1546
123rd Battalion	cap & off col ORs m/col	)70-3-123)	27 Dec 15, 683-167-2, Vol 1541
124th Battalion	cap	70-3-124	31 Dec 15, 683-187-2, Vol 1543
125th Battalion	cap & col	125	25 Feb 16, 683-259-1, Vol 1548
126th Battalion	cap & col	126A	30 Dec 15, 683-211-2, Vol 1545
127th Battalion	cap & col	127A	14 Jan 16, 683-212-1, Vol 1545
128th Battalion	cap & m/col	128	23 Dec 15, 683-198-1, Vol 1544
129th Battalion	cap & col	129	6 May 16, 683-199-1, Vol 1544
130th Battalion	cap & col	130	23 Feb 16, 683-210-3, Vol 1545

132nd Battalion	cap & col	132	31 Dec 15, 683-213-1, Vol 1545
133rd Battalion	cap & col	133	26 Feb 16, 683-268-1, Vol 1639
134th Battalion	glen & m/col	134	15 Jan 16, 683-177-3, Vol 1542
135th Battalion	cap & col	135A	30 Mar 16, 683-171-2, Vol 1542
138th Battalion	cap & col	138A	19 Jan 16, 683-232-1, Vol 1546
139th Battalion	cap & col	139	29 Jan 16, 683-166-1, Vol 1541
141st Battalion	cap & col	141	8 Apr 16, 683-169-1, Vol 1542
144th Battalion	cap & col	144A	24 Jan 16, 683-209-1, Vol 1545
148th Battalion	cap & col	148	9 Dec 15, 683-178-1, Vol 1542
149th Battalion	cap & col	149A	5 Jun 16, 683-330-1, Vol 1667
150th Battalion	cap & col	150	24 Jan 16, 683-188-1, Vol 1543
151st Battalion	cap & col	151A	28 Jan 16, 683-239-1, Vol 1547
152nd Battalion	cap & col	152	27 May 16, 683-332-1, Vol 1667
154th Battalion	cap & col	154	19 Jan 16, 683-234-1, Vol 1546
155th Battalion	cap & col	155A	27 Dec 15, 683-181-1, Vol 1543
156th Battalion	cap & col	156A	16 Feb 16, 683-231-1, Vol 1546
157th Battalion	cap & col	157A	5 Jun 16, 683-342-1, Vol 1672
159th Battalion	cap & col	159	26 May 16, 683-269-2, Vol 1639
160th Battalion	cap & col	160	8 Mar 16, 683-262-2, Vol 1548
162nd Battalion	cap & col	162	4 Mar 16, 683-277-1, Vol 1643
163rd Battalion	cap & col	163	20 Jan 16, 683-229-1, Vol 1546
164th Battalion	cap & col	164	23 Mar 16, 683-293-1, Vol 1651
165th Battalion	cap & col	165	5 Jul 16, 683-316-1, Vol 1662
166th Battalion	cap & col	166	14 Feb 16, 683-252-1, Vol 1547
169th Battalion	cap & col	169A	9 Feb 16, 683-246-1, Vol 1547
170th Battalion	cap & m/col	170A	25 Feb 16, 683-249-1, Vol 1547
171st Battalion	cap & col	171	13 Apr 16, 683-227-1, Vol 1546
173rd Battalion	glen & col	173A	24 Feb 16, 683-258-1, Vol 1548
174th Battalion	glen/bal & m/col	174	16 Nov 16, 683-266-2, Vol 1565
175th Battalion	cap & col	175B	25 Apr 16, 683-324-1, Vol 1665
176th Battalion	cap & col	176	1 Jun 16, 683-250-3, Vol 1547
178th Battalion	cap & m/col	178A	3 Mar 16, 683-248-1, Vol 1547

179th Battalion	glen/bal & col	179	24 Apr 16, 683-267-2, Vol 1565
180th Battalion	cap & col	180A	16 Feb 16, 683-253-1, Vol 1548
181st Battalion	cap & col	181	17 May 16, 683-339-1, Vol 1670
182nd Battalion	cap & col	182	23 Mar 16, 683-285-1, Vol 1647
183rd Battalion	m/col	183A	23 Mar 16, 683-287-1, Vol 1648
185th Battalion	bal & col (both styles of col)	185A	1 Apr 16, 683-254-2, Vol 1548
187th Battalion	cap & col	187	23 May 16, 683-341-1, Vol 1672
190th Battalion	cap & col	190	12 May 16, 683-333-1, Vol 1668
191st Battalion	cap & col	191	12 Jul 16, 683-369-1, Vol 1682
192nd Battalion	cap & col	192	3 Jul 16, 683-370-1, Vol 1682
194th Battalion	glen & col	194	18 Jul 16, 683-296-4, Vol 1652
195th Battalion	cap & col	195	11 Apr 16, 683-297-1, Vol 1652
198th Battalion	cap & m/col	198A	30 Jun 16, 34-4-7 (Vol 4), Vol 4348
	off m/col	198C	25 Jun 17, B-72-33, Vol 2688* (683-292-1, Vol 1650 missing)
199th Battalion	cap & col	199B	28 Jun 16, 683-282-1, Vol 1645
	cap & col	199A	17 Nov 16, 683-282, Vol 1645
200th Battalion	cap & col	200	cited as 19 Apr 16, 683-298-1, Vol 1653, letter not on file
202nd Battalion	cap & col	202	29 Mar 16, 683-276-2, Vol 1642
203rd Battalion	col	203	6 May 16, 683-295-2, Vol 1651
204th Battalion	cap & col	204A	28 Jun 16, 683-375-2, Vol 1684
205th Battalion - see Machine Gun			
206th Battalion	cap & m/col	206	10 Apr 16, 683-263-1, Vol 1564
207th Battalion	cap & col	207A	6 Apr 16, 683-307-1, Vol 1655
209th Battalion	cap & col	209	10 Jul 16, 683-312-2, Vol 1658
210th Battalion	cap & col	210	8 Jul 16, 683-388-1, Vol 1688
211th Battalion	cap & col	211A	11 July 16, 683-334-1, Vol 1668
212th Battalion	cap & col	212B	8 Mar 16, 683-289-1, Vol 1648, approval of withdrawn 26 Apr 16
	cap & col	212A	7 Jul 16, 683-289-1, Vol 1648
213th Battalion	cap & col	213A	5 Jul 16, 683-338-1, Vol 1669
214th Battalion	cap & m/col	214	27 May 16, 683-340-1, Vol 1670

215th Battalion	cap & col	215	4 Apr 16, 683-281-1, Vol 1645
216th Battalion	cap & col	216A	12 Apr 16, 683-251-1, Vol 1547
217th Battalion	cap & col	217	12 May 16, 683-336-1, Vol 1669
218th Battalion	cap & col	218	1 Jun 16, 683-284-2, Vol 1646
219th Battalion	bal & col (both styles of col)	219A	25 Apr 16, 683-299-2, Vol 1653
220th Battalion	cap	220	21 Mar 16, 683-290-1, Vol 1649
221st Battalion	cap & col	221	13 Apr 16, 683-300-1, Vol 1653
222nd Battalion	cap	222A	10 Apr 16, 683-301-1, Vol 1654
223rd Battalion	cap & col	223	25 Apr 16, 683-323-1, Vol 1664
224th Battalion - see Forestry			
226th Battalion	cap & col	226A	10 Apr 16, 683-317-1, Vol 1663
227th Battalion	cap & col	227	10 Jul 16, 683-368-1, Vol 1682
228th Battalion	cap & col	228	28 Aug 16, 683-392-1, Vol 1690
229th Battalion	cap & col	229	29 Apr 16, 683-326-1, Vol 1665
230th Battalion also see Forestry	cap & col	230A	1 Oct 16, 683-314-2, Vol 1659
232nd Battalion	cap & m/col	232	28 Jun 16, 683-385-1, Vol 1686
233rd Battalion	cap & col	233A	6 Apr 16, 683-309-1, Vol 1657
234th Battalion	cap & col	234	26 May 16, 683-354-1, Vol 1676
235th Battalion	cap & col	235A	19 Jul 16, 683-364-1, Vol 1679
238th Battalion - see Forestry			
239th Battalion - see Railway Troops			
240th Battalion	cap & col	240	7 Jul 16, 683-386-1, Vol 1686
241st Battalion	glen & m/col	241	cited as 4 Nov 16, 683-387-2, Vol 1687, file is missing
242nd Battalion - see Forestry			
248th Battalion	cap & col	248	20 Apr 17, 683-502-1, Vol 1724
249th Battalion	cap & col	249*	27 Apr 17, 683-495-1, Vol 1720 * approved with the name "Saskatchewan" substituted for the words "Heads up"
250th Battalion	cap & col	250	13 Apr 17, 683-468-1, Vol 1711

251st Battalion	cap	251*	) 26 Jan 17, 683-441-1, Vol 1706
	col	251-41*	) *approved without subtitle
			"Goodfellows"
253rd Battalion	glen & col	253A	9 Feb 17, 683-475-1, Vol 1713
254th Battalion	cap & m/col	254	18 Jan 17, 683-472-1, Vol 1712
255th Battalion	cap & col	255	19 Jan 17, 683-479-2, Vol 1714
256th Battalion - see Railway Troops			
257th Battalion - see Railway Troops			
259th & 256th	cap	259/260	) 17 Sep 18, 762-26-1, Vol 2011
Battalions	col	C/259	)
	col	C/260	)

Reinforcing Companies

No 1 Jewish			
Infantry Company	cap & col	261	25 Jan 17, 683-498-1, Vol 1723
No 1 Independent			
Infantry Company	cap	27	10 Feb 17, 683-3-7, Vol 1507
			(granted permission to wear 27th
			Battalion cap badge)
University of Toronto			
Overseas Training	cap & col	264	16 May 16, 34-4-7 (Vol 2),
Company			Vol 4347, file 7429-5-8 not
			located

Artillery

Royal Canadian	cap & col	110-1-1	1 Aug 18, GRO 4663
Horse Artillery			(badges originally approved by
Brigade			GO 175/1905)
Canadian Field	) cap	140-1-3	26 Apr 18, CEF (Canada) RO 492
Artillery	) col	grenade	1 Aug 18, GRO 4663
Canadian Garrison	)		(cap badge originally approved as
Artillery	)		a pouch badge in 1907 Dress
			Regs)
56th Depot Battery	cap	145-3-56B	7 Jun 16, 683-321-1, Vol 1664
58th Depot Battery	cap	145-3-58	6 Jul 16, 683-141-5, Vol 1540
79th Depot Battery	cap	145-3-79A	21 Sep 16, 683-415-1, Vol 1699
		(style B)	
No 3 Battery Siege			
Siege Artillery	cap & col	150-1-3A	20 Dec 15, 683-184-1, Vol 1568

No 6 Battery Siege Artillery	cap & col	150-3-9B	1 Jun 16, 683-345-3, Vol 1673
McGill Overseas Siege Artillery Draft	cap	150-3-9B	25 Apr 17, 683-345-3, Vol 1673, permission granted to wear badge of No 6 Siege Battery
No 10 Depot Battery Siege Artillery	cap	150-1-10	9 Feb 17, 683-480-1, Vol 1714
3rd Divisional Ammunition Column	cap	150-9-3	17 Feb 16, 683-80-1, Vol 1529
4th Divisional Ammunition Column	cap	150-9-4	26 May 16, 683-328-1, Vol 1666

Cavalry and Mounted Rifles

Royal Canadian Dragoons	cap & m/col	10-1-1	9 Nov 16, 4-2-16, Vol 8* 1 Aug 18, GRO 4663 (badges originally approved GO 50/1908)
Lord Strathcona's Horse (Royal Canadians)	cap & col	10-1-3	9 Nov 16, 4-2-16, Vol 8* 1 Aug 18, GRO 4663 (badges originally approved GO 2/1912)
Fort Garry Horse	cap & col	figure 20	13 Jun 18, C-1013-33 (vol 1), Vol 2744*l 1 Aug 18, GRO 4663
34th Fort Garry Horse, Service Squadron	cap & col	10-1-5	(badges originally approved GO 157/1913)
Canadian Light Horse A Squadron (19th Alberta Dragoons)	cap & m/col	10-5-5	17 Feb 17, B-4-3, Vol 884* 1 Aug 18, GRO 4663 (badges of parent militia regiment originally approved GO 80/1908, amended by GO 5/1911)
B Squadron (1st Hussars)	cap & m/col	10-5-3	17 Feb 17, B-4-3, Vol 884* 1 Aug 18, GRO 4663 (badges of parent militia regiment never approved in GOs)

C Squadron (16th Light Horse)	cap & m/col	10-5-7	1 Aug 18, GRO 4663 (badges of parent militia regiment originally approved GO 100/1907)
6th Regiment CMR	cap & m/col	10-7-6	19 Jun 15, 683-94-2, Vol 1532
9th Regiment CMR	cap & m/col	10-7-9	12 Jun 15, 683-85-3, Vol 1530

Engineers and Pioneers

Canadian Engineers	cap col	70-1-1 grenade	) 1 Aug 18, GRO 4663) (cap badges originally approved GO 277/1905)
2nd Pioneer Bn	cap & col	70-3-2	27 Nov 15, 683-152-1, Vol 1541
4th Pioneer Bn	cap & col	70-3-4	cited as 15 Apr 16, 683-313-2, Vol 1659, file is missing
5th Pioneer Bn	cap & m/col	70-3-5	13 Apr 16, 683-304-1, Vol 1654

107th Pioneer Bn - see Infantry
123rd Pioneer Bn - see Infantry
124th Pioneer Bn - see Infantry

Labour Group

1st Infantry Works Company	cap & col	70-13-1	28 Oct 18, Q28/56, cited in 29 Oct 18, Folder 1, File 5, Vol 4452
2nd Infantry Works Company	cap & col	70-13-2	28 Oct 18, Q28/56, cited in 29 Oct 18, Folder 1, File 5, Vol 4452
3rd Infantry Works Company	cap & col	70-13-3	28 Oct 18, Q28/56, cited in 29 Oct 18, Folder 1, File 5, Vol 4452
4th Infantry Works Company	cap & col	70-13-4	28 Oct 18, Q28/56, cited in 29 Oct 18, Folder 1, File 5, Vol 4452

Signal Service (part of Canadian Engineers)

Canadian Signal Service	cap & col	100-1-1	(badges of Canadian Signal Corps originally approved GO 33/1908) (personnel presently wearing above badges are permitted to continue, 2 Sep 17, B-4-3, Vol 884*)
	cap col	70-1-1 grenade	) 3 Jul 17, B-4-3, Vol 884*, to wear) Canadian Engineers badges 1 Aug 18, GRO 4663

Machine Gun Corps

Canadian Machine Gun Corps	cap	45-1-1	7 May 17, GRO 2291 (British Machine Gun Corps badge)
	cap & col	45-1-3/5/7	17 Aug 18, GRO 4798
Eaton's Machine Gun Battery	cap & col	50-3-1	23 Mar 15, 34-4-7 (Vol 1), Vol 4347, file 640-1-4 not located
1st Canadian Motor Machine Gun Brigade	m/col	50-1-1	19 Sep 18, C-1013-33 (Vol 2), Vol 2744*
86th Machine Gun Battalion	cap & col	86	25 Sep 15, 683-133-1, Vol 1539
205th (Machine Gun Depot) Battalion	cap & col	205	1 Apr 16, 683-308-1, Vol 1656 (Requested permission to wear CMGC badges, 28 Sep 17, 34-4-7 (Vol 5), Vol 4348, reply not located).
Canadian Machine Gun Depot	cap & col	86	(wore the approved 86th Machine Gun Battalion badges, Folder 39, File 8, Vol 4687*, later replaced by British Machine Gun Corps badges)

Service Corps

Canadian Army Service Corps	cap & col	95-1-1	Dress Regs dated 10 Dec 16, D-157-33, Vol 2765* (badges originally approved GO 32/1908)

Medical Service

Canadian Medical Corps	cap & col	85-1-1	Dress Regs dated 10 Dec 16, D-157-33, Vol 2765* (authorized sealed pattern cited 26 Mar 17, 47-4-3, Vol 4260)
No 9 Stationary Hospital	cap & col	85-3-9	12 May 16, 683-335-1, Vol 1669

Chaplain Service

Chaplains of the CEF	cap & col	80-1-3	28 Dec 16, D-30-1, Vol 416* (badges worn by Imperial Chaplains, originally approved GO 231/1905)

Canadian Chaplain Service	cap & col	80-1-1	12 Oct 17, C-23-43 (Vol 1) Vol 3298*
Military Police			
Canadian Military Police Corps	cap col	60-1-1A C.M.P.C	) 27 May 18, 96-11-69, Vol 6403)
Corps Cyclists			
No 2 Divisional Cyclist Company	cap & col	20-3-2A	6 Apr 15, 34-4-7 (Vol 2), Vol 4347, file 83-44-1 not located
No 3 Divisional Cyclist Company	cap & col	20-3-3	22 Jan 16, 34-4-7 (Vol 2), Vol 4347, file 683-44-1 not located
Canadian Corps Cyclist Battalion	cap & col	20-1-1	18 Dec 17, B-4-3 (Vol 2), Vol 884*
Forestry Corps			
122nd Battalion	cap & col	122A	22 Feb 17, 683-236-1, Vol 1546
224th Canadian Forestry Battalion	cap & col	30-3-4	cited as 25 Feb 16, 683-286-4, Vol 1648, letter not on file
230th Forestry Battalion	cap & col	230B	29 Mar 17, 683-314-2, Vol 1659
238th Canadian Forestry Battalion	cap & col	30-3-5	7 Jun 16, 683-365-1, Vol 1680
242nd Forestry Battalion	cap & col	242	2 Oct 16, 683-366-2, Vol 1681
Forestry Company MD No 10	cap & col	30-5-82	23 Mar 17, 683-523-1, Vol 1729
Canadian Forestry Corps	cap & col	30-1-1A	25 Jun 18, File 5, Vol 4502*
Railway Troops			
Corps of Canadian Railway Troops	cap & col	Figure 39	28 Oct 18, Folder 1, File 2, Vol 4472* (badges never made)
No 1 Construction Battalion	cap & col	65-3-1	11 July 16, 683-347-1, Vol 1673

No 2 Construction Battalion	cap & col	65-3-2	4 Nov 16, 683-401-4, Vol 1695
143rd Railway Construction Battalion - see Infantry			
218th Railway Construction Battalion - see Infantry			
228th Railway Construction Battalion - see Infantry			
239th Overseas Railway Construction Battalion	cap & col	239	24 Jul 16, 683-360-1, Vol 1677
256th Overseas Railway Construction Battalion	cap & col	256	1 Feb 17, 683-494-2, Vol 1719
257th Overseas Railway Construction Battalion	cap & col	257A	18 Jan 17, 683-493-1, Vol 1718
No 1 Section Skilled Railway Employees	cap & col	65-11-1	30 Jan 17, 683-492-1, Vol 1718

Tank Corps

1st Tank Battalion	cap & m/col	75-3-1	17 Apr 1918, 683-782-1, Vol 1794
Canadian Tank Corps	cap	75-1-1A	17 Feb 19, B-72-33, Vol 2688*

Other Corps and Services, Miscellaneous Units

Canadian Army Dental Corps	cap & col	105-1-1B	22 July 15, B-2-8, Vol 1545*
Canadian Ordnance Corps	cap & col	125-1-1	(badges originally approved GO 36/1904)

Canadian Arms
  Inspection and
  Repair Department
	cap & col	125-3-1	31 Oct 15, 4-2-18, Vol 8*

Canadian Army Veterinary Corps	cap & m/col	5-1-3A/B	(badges originally approved GO 65/1912)
	cap & col	5-1-1	Dress Regs dated 10 Dec 16, D-157-33, Vol 2765*

Canadian Army Pay Corps	cap & m/col	90-1-1	(badges originally approved 1907 Dress Regs)
	cap & m/col	90-1-3	Corps Dress Regs dated 17 Sep 18, D-157-33, Vol 2765*
Canadian Postal Corps	cap & col	130-1-1	1 Aug 18, GRO 4663 (badges originally approved GO 175/1912)
Corps of Military Staff Clerks	cap & col	15-3-1	(badges originally approved GO 51/1908)
Canadian School of Musketry	cap & m/col	17-7-1	(badges originally approved GO 65/1912)
Canadian Army Gymnastic Staff	cap	15-7-3	Orders for Dress, Warrant Officers and NCOs dated 1 Jan 16, 17-1-60 (Vol 1), Vol 4511
Bayonet Fighting and Physical Training Instructors	cap	crossed swords	11 Oct 16, HQ Circular Letter, cited 23 Jan 17, 17-1-62 (Vol 2), Vol 4511, re Instructors in Canada
Department of The General Auditor	cap & col	15-5-1	Department Dress Regs dated 29 Nov 16, D-169-33, Vol 2766*
Canadian Garrison Regiment	cap & col	35-1-1	7 Jun 18, 96-11-97, Vol 1201
Khaki University	cap & col	165-1-1	4 Feb 19, B-72-33, Vol 2688*
General Issue	cap & collar	maple leaf	29 Mar 15, MO 164 (worn by units not having special badges. Badges originally approved GO 65/1912 for Staff Orderly Service)

Notes

1. Type: col = collar; m/col = matching collars; bal = balmoral; glen = glengarry; off = officers.

2. Design: references are to Cross' books unless otherwise indicated.

3. Approval: contains hand-written date approved by the Minister of Militia or other authority, file number, National Archives of Canada volume (Vol) number. Volumes are in RG24 or if indicated by * are in RG9III. If approval date was not available, the date of the letter advising of approval is given. If the file was missing or the approval letter was not on file, the date used was that cited in the table *Special Designations and Badges of Infantry Battalions* found in various RG24 battalion badge files.

4. It was decided by the Director of Ordnance Services OMFC 25 March 1918 to supply regimental design collar badges instead of those approved in GRO 4663 (C-33-43 (Vol 1), Vol 3298*).

Appendix 3
Approvals Claimed For Badges and Shoulder Titles

Unit	Type[1]	Design[2]	Remarks[3]
Infantry			
11th Battalion	cap & col	11	Claims approved by HQ Canadians, London, Summer 1916 (*Historical Record,* Folder 89, File 19, Vol 4708*)
28th Battalion	cap & col	28A	OC claims approved early 1915 in Winnipeg (Letter 21 May 1917, Folder 55, File 2, Vol 4694*) (Nothing on 683-66-2, Vol 1525)
30th Battalion	cap & col	30B	OC claims approved by GOC CTD Mar 15 (Letter 25 Nov 16, Folder 56, File 61, Vol 4694*) (Nothing on 683-19-3, Vol 1513)
32nd Battalion	cap & col	32	OC claims approved by AA&QMG Shorncliffe 15 Apr 15 (Letter 20 Nov 16, Folder 56, File 11, Vol 4694*) (Nothing on 683-2-5, Vol 1507)
38th Battalion	cap & col	38	Claims approved Mar 15 by Minister of Militia (Letter 24 May 17, Folder 57, File 2, Vol 4694*) (Nothing on 683-16-14, Vol 1512)
49th Battalion	cap & col	49B	OC claims approved Aug or Sep 16 (Letter 21 May 17, Folder 60, File 2, Vol 4696*) (Nothing on 683-20-2, Vol 1513)
70th Battalion	cap & col	70	OC claims approved by Militia HQ Ottawa. (Letter 24 Nov 16, Folder 63, File 16, Vol 4697*) (Nothing on 683-191-4, Vol 1543)
105th Battalion	cap & col	105	OC claims approved by authorities in Canada (Letter 22 Nov 16, Folder 68, File 57, Vol 4699*) (Nothing on 683-168-3, Vol 1560)

110th Battalion	cap & col	110A	OC claims approved by HQ Ottawa Jan 16 (Folder 69, File 12, Vol 4699*) (683-230-2, Vol 1573 is missing)
143rd Battalion	cap & col	143	OC claims approved by HQ Ottawa (Letter 25 May 17 Folder 73, File 10, Vol 4701*) (Nothing on 683-348-6, Vol 1674)
146th Battalion	cap & col	146	Claims approved Dec 15 by HQ Ottawa (Folder 118A, File 24, Vol 4720*) (Nothing on 683-186-7, Vol 1568)
147th Battalion	cap & col	147A	Claims approved by HQ Ottawa (Memo received 26 April 17, Folder 73, File 19, Vol 4701*) (Nothing on 683-240-7, Vol 1584)
184th Battalion	cap & col	184	OC claims approved Feb 16 by Militia Council (Folder 77, File 11, Vol 4702*) (Nothing on 683-235-5, Vol 1582)
188th Battalion	cap & col	188	Claims approved Mar 16 by HQ Ottawa (Letter 22 Mar 17, Folder 77, File 20, Vol 4702*) (Nothing on 683-283-7, Vol 1646)
189th Battalion	cap & col	189	OC claims approved 11 Jan 16 by HQ Ottawa (Letter 20 Nov 16, Folder 77, File 23, Vol 4702*) (Nothing on 683-363-5, Vol 1679)
198th Battalion	cap & col	198B	OC claims design approved Jul 16 by Colonel of the Buffs and HM The King (Letter 11 Jun 17, Folder 78, File 24, Vol 4703*)
245th Battalion	cap & col	245	OC claims approved 21 Oct 16 by DAA&QMG MD No 4 (Letter 28 May 17, Folder 83, File 2, Vol 4705*) (683-398-1, Vol 1694 missing)

Pioneers

3rd Pioneer Battalion	s/title	2 over CANADIAN over PIONEERS (yellow on black)	OC claims approved July 1916 by Divisional Commander (Letter 16 May 1917, Folder 92, File 6, Vol 4709*)

Medical Service

No 9 Field Ambulance	s/title	85-7-9	OC claims approved Feb 1916 (Letter 20 May 1917, Folder 107, File 19, Vol 4715*) (Nothing located on HQ Files)
No 10 Field Ambulance	s/title	85-7-10	OC claims approved by GOC MD 10 (RG9IIIC.10, Folder 1, File 3, Vol 4554*) (Nothing located on HQ Files)
No 15 Field Ambulance	cap & col	85-7-2B	OC claims approved by HQ Ottawa (Letter 16 Apr 16, Folder 108, File 4, Vol 4715* (HQ File not located)

Notes

1. Type: col = collar

2. Design: references are to Cross' books unless otherwise indicated

3. Remarks: volumes are in RG24 or if indicated by * are in RG9III.

Appendix 4
Approval of Shoulder Titles

Unit	Design[1]	Approval[2]
Infantry		
Royal Canadian Regiment	R C R	1 Aug 18, GRO 4663
Princess Patricia's Canadian Light Infantry	P.P.C.L.I., (white on red)	1 Aug 18, GRO 4663
5th Battalion	5A-93	1 Aug 18, GRO 4663
13th Battalion	R H C	1 Aug 18, GRO 4663
14th Battalion	R.M.R over CANADA	1 Aug 18, GRO 4663 (Permission to continue wearing was requested 20 Mar 16, Folder 6, File 3, Vol 3876*)
16th Battalion	CANADIAN over SCOTTISH	1 Aug 18, GRO 4663
24th Battalion	V R C	1 Aug 18, GRO 4663
42nd Battalion	R H C	1 Aug 18, GRO 4663
73rd Battalion	73rd R.H. of C.	12 Aug 15, 683-102-1, Vol 1533
111th Battalion	111th over CANADA, (white on khaki)	3 Jul 16, 683-377-1, Vol 1685 (never implemented, 14 Nov 16, 683-377-1, Vol 1685)
166th Battalion	unknown lettering on khaki	22 Jun 16, 683-252-1, Vol 1547
194th Battalion	194-93 & 95	18 Jul 16, 683-296-4, Vol 1652
199th Battalion	199A-95	17 Nov 16, 683-282-1, Vol 1645
207th Battalion	CANADA over 207, (red on black)	15 Jul 16, 683-307-1, Vol 1655
217th Battalion	both metal & cloth	29 Sept 16, 683-336-1, Vol 1669
220th Battalion	220-95	28 Mar 17, 683-290-1, Vol 1649
228th Battalion	228 over CANADA 228-91	) 28 Aug 16, 683-392-1, Vol 1690)
230th Battalion	230A-93	1 Oct 16, 683-314-2, Vol 1659

253rd Battalion	253A-93	9 Feb 17, 683-475-1, Vol 1713
255th Battalion	QOR over 255 over CANADA, (red on khaki)	28 Dec 16, 34-4-7 (Vol 4), Vol 4348

Artillery

Royal Canadian Horse Artillery Brigade	R C H A	Dress Regs dated 10 Dec 16, D-157-33, Vol 2765* 1 Aug 18, GRO 4663
Canadian Field Artillery	C.F.A	Dress Regs dated 10 Dec 16, D-157-33, Vol 2765* 1 Aug 18, GRO 4663
Canadian Garrison Artillery	C.G.A	1 Aug 18, GRO 4663
64th Depot Battery	145-3-64A-91	9 Feb 17, 683-408-2, Vol 1698
79th Depot Battery	145-3-79A-91	11 Jul 17, 683-415-1, Vol 1699
No 6 Siege Battery	Nº 6 McGILL over BATTERY	1 Jun 16, 683-345-3, Vol 1673

Cavalry and Mounted Rifles

Royal Canadian Dragoons	R.C.D	1 Aug 18, GRO 4663
Lord Strathcona's Horse (Royal Canadians)	STRATHCONA'S	1 Aug 18, GRO 4663
Fort Garry Horse	F G H	1 Aug 18, GRO 4663
Canadian Light Horse	C.L.H	1 Aug 18, GRO 4663
9th Regiment CMR	10-7-9	12 Jun 15, 683-85-3, Vol 1530

Engineers and Pioneers

Canadian Engineers	C.E. C E, (blue on red)	15 Jun 16, 4-2-18, Vol 8* Dress Regs dated 10 Dec 16, D-157-33, Vol 2765* 1 Aug 18, GRO 4663
Engineer Training Depot	C.E., SIGNAL	13 May 16, 96-11-60, Vol 6403
5th Pioneer Bn	5 over PIONEERS over CANADA, (bronze on khaki)	1 Nov 16, 683-304-1, Vol 1654

Machine Gun Corps

86th Machine Gun Battalion	86-93	3 Nov 15, 683-133-1, Vol 1539

Medical Service

Canadian Army Medical Corps	C.A.M.C	30 Apr 15, 683-1-4, Vol 1485
No 6 Stationary Hospital	LAVAL*	7 Oct 15, 683-126-1, Vol 1551 *Worn with regular shoulder titles

Railway Troops

No 1 Construction Battalion	CONSTR	11 Jul 16, 683-347-1, Vol 1673
Canadian Railway Troops Depot (Canada)	C.R.T.	12 Aug 18, 34-4-7 (vol 5), Vol 4348
239th Overseas Railway Battalion	239 over CANADA	24 Jul 16, 683-360-1, Vol 1677 (different styles of titles for Construction Officers and ORs)

Garrison Regiment

Canadian Garrison Regiment	C.G.R	)
1st Battalion	1BN	)
2nd Battalion	2BN	)
3rd Battalion	3BN	)
4th Battalion	4BN	) July 18, 96-11-97, Vol 1201
5th Battalion	5BN	)
6th Battalion	6BN	)
10th Battalion	10BN	)
11th Battalion	11BN	)
12th Battalion	12BN	)
13th Battalion	13BN	)

Other Corps and Services, Miscellaneous Units

Canadian Signal Service	SIGNAL	13 May 16, 96-11-60, Vol 6403 26 April 18, CEF (Canada) RO 492
Canadian Army Service Corps	C.A.S.C	30 Apr 15, 683-1-4, Vol 1485
Canadian Army Dental Corps	C.A.D.C	Dress Regs dated 10 Dec 16, D-157-33, Vol 2765*

Canadian Ordnance Corps	C.O.C	Dress Regs dated 10 Dec 16, D-157-33, Vol 2765*
Canadian Army Veterinary Corps	C.A.V.C	Dress Regs dated 10 Dec 16, D-157-33, Vol 2765* (title originally approved GO 66/1912)
Corps of Military Staff Clerks	C.M.S.C	(title originally approved GO 77/1916)
No 1 Divisional Cyclist Company	CYCLISTS	20 Apr 15, 4-2-8, Vol 8*
Canadian Army Dental Corps	C.A.D.C	Dress Regs dated 10 Dec 16, D-157-33, Vol 2765*
Canadian Military Police	C.M.F.P C.M.M.P	Dress Regs dated 10 Dec 16, D-157-33, Vol 2765*
Canadian Tank Corps	T.C	9 Apr 18, GRO 3776
Canadian Army Gymnastic Staff	C.A.G.S	Staff Dress Regs dated 1 Jan 16, 17-1-60 (Vol l), Vol 4511
Depot Battalions	Appendix 14	) 26 Apr 18, CEF (Canada) RO 492) and 9 May 18 CEF (Canada) RO 541

Note

1. Design: references are to Cross' books unless titles are described

2. Approval: contains hand-written date approved by the Minister of Militia or other authority, file number, National Archives of Canada volume (Vol) number. Volumes are in RG24 or if indicated by * are in RG9III. If approval date was not available, the date of the letter advising of approval is given.

Appendix 5
Approval of Badges Denied

Unit	Type[1]	Design[2]	Rejected[3]
Infantry			
10th Battalion	cap & m/col	10A	9 Nov 15 approval requested, Folder 6, File 2, Vol 3876*. 27 Jan 16 denied request that government supply, 4-2-18, Vol 8*
53rd Battalion	cap & col	unknown	15 Feb 16 (design did not contain "Overseas", 683-87-3, Vol 1530)
55th Battalion	cap & col	unknown	15 Sep 15 (design did not contain "Overseas" 683-41-2, Vol 1520)
56th Battalion	cap & col	unknown	2 Jul 15 (design did not contain "Overseas", 683-89-1, Vol 1531)
82nd Battalion	col	C/82	6 Jan 16 (request denied, 683-222-1, Vol 1546)
142nd Battalion	cap	Figure 81	29 Jan 16 (design not a maple leaf and did not contain "Overseas", 683-233-1, Vol 1546)
151st Battalion	cap & col	151B	19 Apr 16 (design error by maker. Request to use denied, 683-239-1, Vol 1547)
201st Battalion	cap & col	201A	13 Apr 16 (approval held in abeyance. No further action, 683-257-2, Vol 1548)
208th Battalion	cap & col	208A	3 Jul & 8 Nov 16 (design requested twice. OC did not reply, 34-4-7 (Vol 4), Vol 4348)
236th Battalion	cap	236B	18 Oct 17 (designation "MacLean Kilties of America, Sir Sam's Own" not approved, 683-393-3, Vol 1691)
247th Battalion	cap	on file	17 March 16 (design rejected, 683-438-1, Vol 1705)
Depot Battalions			
1st Depot Battalion Nova Scotia Regiment	cap & col	25-5-1	22 Nov 17 (circular letter 312 sent to OC, 129-6-3-5, Vol 4555)

1st Depot Battalion 1st Quebec Regiment	cap & col	25-11-1A/B	23 Jan 18 (Minister does not concur in the issue of special badges, 683-670-4, Vol 1778)
3rd Depot Battalion 2nd Quebec Regiment	cap & col	unknown	16 Jul 18 (special badges for Depot Battalions disapproved, 683-817-1, Vol 1799)
1st Depot Battalion Eastern Ontario Regiment	cap & col	Figure 81	1 Oct 17 (units will be issued with maple leaf badges, 683-655-1, Vol 1775)
2nd Depot Battalion Eastern Ontario Regiment	cap & col	unknown	24 Apr 18 (special badges for Depot Battalions disapproved, 683-673-5, Vol 1779)
1st Depot Battalion Western Ontario Regiment	cap & col	unknown	24 Apr 18 (special badges for Depot Battalions disapproved, 683-672-5, Vol 1779)

Cavalry and Mounted Rifles

4th Regiment CMR	cap	10-7-4B	4 Feb 15 (special badges for units of the CEF are not permitted, 683-12-1, Vol 1511)
5th Regiment CMR	cap & m/col	on file (not 10-7-5)	29 Jun 15 (design did not contain "Overseas", 683-42-1, Vol 1520)
7th Regiment CMR	cap	figure 22	21 Apr 15 (design did not contain "Overseas", 47-3-27, Vol 4260) (File 683-49-2 not located)
Depot Regiment Canadian Mounted Rifles	cap & col	10-9-1	2 Jun, 4 July, 24 Aug 16, (the maple leaf should be sufficient for any Depot, 683-361-1, Vol 1678)

Artillery

65th Depot Battery	cap	145-3-65	31 Jan 18 (approved pattern for general service may be worn, 683-59-5, Vol 1677)
66th Depot Battery	cap	unknown	11 Jul 16 (specimen not received 683-373-1, Vol 1683)
70th Depot Battery	cap	145-3-70	5 Jan 18 (there should be no alteration in the badges issued to CEF Artillery Units, 34-4-47 (Vol 5), Vol 4348)

| No 1 Battery Siege Artillery Reinforcements | cap | 140-1-2 | 23 Feb 16 (cannot use militia artillery badge instead of maple leaf badge, 683-264-1, Vol 1564) |

Engineers and Pioneers

| 1st Pioneer Bn | cap & col | unknown | 9 Sep 15 (design did not contain "Overseas", 683-129-2, Vol 1539) |

Machine Gun Corps

| New Brunswick Machine Gun Draft | cap | Figure 81 | 7 Oct 16 (no special badge approved for Machine Gun Detachments or Drafts, 640-1-10, Vol 6533) |

Canadian Garrison Regiment

| 4th Battalion | cap | 35-5-4 | 20 Jun 18 (arrangements made for suitable badge for all CGRs 683-792-2, Vol 1795) |
| 6th Battalion | cap | unknown | 25 Sep 18 (pattern of badges for CGR already approved 683-793-3, Vol 1796) |

Notes

1. Type: col = collar.

2. Design: references are to Cross' books unless otherwise indicated.

3. Rejected: date of letter rejecting the design and reasons given for rejection; volumes are in RG24 or if indicated by * are in RG9III.

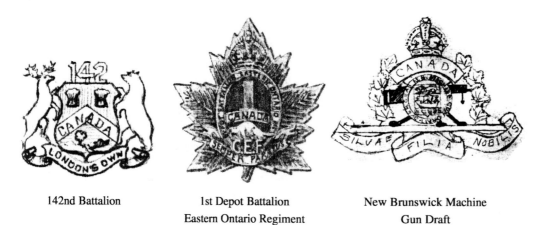

142nd Battalion   1st Depot Battalion   New Brunswick Machine
                              Eastern Ontario Regiment   Gun Draft

Figure 81 *Designs of badges for which approval was denied*

NAC RG24

Appendix 6
Approval of Shoulder Titles Denied

Unit	Design[1]	Rejected[2]
Infantry		
76th Battalion	76 CANADIANS (worsted)	27 Sep 15 (all infantry units issued with "Infantry" "Numeral" and Canada badge, 683-135-1, Vol 1539)
77th Battalion	77th INF over OTTAWA over CANADA	20 Jun 16 (No action, unit embarked for overseas, 683-79-2, Vol 1529)
79th Battalion	unknown	20 Apr 16 ("Canada" with numeral and branch of service only approved, 683-140-2, Vol 1540)
89th Battalion	89-93	8 Dec 15 (shoulder badges will be the same as that issued to all units of the CEF, 683-157-1, Vol 1541)
96th Battalion	OVERSEAS CANADIAN BATTALION over 96 (on a plate)	26 Mar 16 (title must be word "Canada", 683-224-3, Vol 1546)
106th Battalion	106 over N.S.R over CANADA	26 Apr 16 (only universal shoulder badge worn, 683-256-1, Vol 1548)
109th Battalion	unknown	24 Apr 16 (similar designs not approved, 683-182-1, Vol 1543)
117th Battalion	unknown	19 May 16 (use of designs other than universal "Canada" cannot be permitted, 683-265-2, Vol 1565)
160th Battalion	BRUCE, (white on red)	2 Jun 16 (design does not have word "Canada", 683-262-2, Vol 1548)
168th Battalion	168 CANADA	20 Jun 16 (not the pattern issued, 47-3-22, Vol 4260)
183rd Battalion	on file	23 Mar 16 (shoulder title should be universal "Canada", 683-287-1, Vol 1648)

195th Battalion	195-93 & 95	14 Apr 16, (only universal "Canada" with numeral approved, 683-297-1, Vol 1652)
229th Battalion	229A-93 & 95	29 Apr 16 (badges approved but not design of title, 683-326-l, Vol 1665)
250th Battalion	250-93	13 Apr 17 (badges approved but not design of title, 683-468-l, Vol 1711)

Artillery

50th Depot Battery	Q over 50CFA	23 Mar 16 (Royal approval required, 683-271-1, Vol 1640)
65th Depot Battery	unknown	31 Jan 18 (only those of approved pattern for general service to be worn, 683-59-5, Vol 1677)
70th Depot Battery	70 BATTERY over CANADA (red on blue)	5 Jan 18 (proper titles are 70 over CFA over CANADA, 34-4-47 (Vol 5), Vol 4348)

Machine Gun Corps

New Brunswick Machine Gun Draft	N.B.M.G.D over CANADA plate	7 Oct 16 (no special title approved for Machine Gun Detachments or Drafts, 640-1-10, Vol 6533)

Notes

1. Design: references are to Cross' books unless titles are described.

2. Rejected: date of letter rejecting the design and reasons for rejection when given, volumes are in RG24.

Appendix 7
Approval of Badges and Shoulder Titles Requested
Reply not Located in Files

Unit	Type[1]	Design[2]	Request Letter[3]
Infantry			
18th Battalion	cap	18B	)
			)
19th Battalion	cap	19B	) 11 Aug 16 (GOC 4th Infantry
			) Brigade to 2nd Canadian Division,
20th Battalion	cap	20A	) Folder 3, File 1, Vol 4099*)
			)
21st Battalion	cap	21	)
50th Battalion	cap & col	50B	22 Jun 17 (B-4-3, Vol 884*)
129th Battalion	s/title	unknown	25 May 16 (34-4-47 (Vol 3), Vol 4347)
168th Battalion	cap	168A	8 Oct 16 (specimens requested for approval, no record of receipt, 47-3-22, Vol 4260) (File 96-11-64 not located)
Artillery			
66th Depot Battery	cap	145-3-66	11 Jul 16 (specimen lost, another requested. No further action, 683-373-1, Vol 1683)

Notes

1. Type: col = collar, s/title = shoulder title.

2. Design: references are to Cross' books unless titles are described.

3. Request Letter: volumes are in RG24 or if indicated by * are in RG9III.

Appendix 8
Source of Supply of Badges and Shoulder Titles
Worn by the Canadian Corps August 1917

Unit	Maker/Possessor of Dies
1st Canadian Division	
1st Battalion	Hicks & Sons, London
2nd Battalion	Henry Jenkins & Son, Birmingham
3rd Battalion	J R Gaunt & Sons, Birmingham
4th Battalion	W J Dingley, Birmingham
5th Battalion	J W Tiptaft & Son, Birmingham (maker)
	Goldsmiths & Silversmiths, London (dies)
7th Battalion	Hicks & Sons, London
8th Battalion	J W Tiptaft & Son, Birmingham
10th Battalion	Hicks & Sons, London
13th Battalion	Henry Jenkins & Son, Birmingham
	Hobson & Sons, London
14th Battalion	Henry Jenkins & Son, Birmingham
15th Battalion	Moore, Taggart & Co., Glasgow
16th Battalion	McDougall, London
3rd Machine Gun Company	George F Hemsley, Montreal
No 1 Field Ambulance	J W Tiptaft & Son, Birmingham (title)
No 3 Field Ambulance	J W Tiptaft & Son, Birmingham (title)
1st Divisional Signals	Alexis David, Paris
2nd Canadian Division	
18th Battalion	Sidney Barron, Folkestone
19th Battalion	J R Gaunt & Sons, Coventry St, London
20th Battalion	badge not approved
21st Battalion	J W Tiptaft & Son, Birmingham
22nd Battalion	Caron Bros, Montreal
24th Battalion	J W Tiptaft & Son, Birmingham
25th Battalion	J R Gaunt & Sons, Birmingham
26th Battalion	G Barron, Folkestone
27th Battalion	D R Dingwall, Winnipeg
	Twigg, Birmingham (C/27)
28th Battalion	Wheeler & Co., London
29th Battalion	Army & Navy Co-operative Society, London
31st Battalion	H Ford, London
2nd Pioneer Battalion	Vaughtons, Birmingham
4th Machine Gun Company	George Jamieson & Sons, Aberdeen
No 4 Field Ambulance	Alfred Constantine, Birmingham

3rd Canadian Division

Royal Canadian Regiment	Smith & Wright, Birmingham
Princess Patricia's Canadian Light Infantry	Goldsmiths & Silversmiths, London
42nd Battalion	Wm Anderson & Sons, Edinburgh (hackles)
	Henry Jenkins & Son, Birmingham
43rd Battalion	Moore, Taggart & Co., Glasgow
49th Battalion	J R Gaunt & Sons, Birmingham
52nd Battalion	J W Tiptaft & Son, Birmingham
58th Battalion	J W Tiptaft & Son, Birmingham
116th Battalion	Miller Bros, London
1st CMR Battalion	J W Tiptaft & Son, Birmingham
2nd CMR Battalion	J W Tiptaft & Son, Birmingham
4th CMR Battalion	J W Tiptaft & Son, Birmingham
5th CMR Battalion	R J Inglis, Montreal
9th Machine Gun Company	Moore, Taggart & Co., Glasgow
123rd Pioneer Battalion	Ellis Bros, Toronto
	J W Tiptaft & Son, Birmingham
36th Battery CFA	J R Gaunt & Sons, Birmingham (title)
No 8 Field Ambulance	Saqui, London
No 10 Field Ambulance	Botty & Lewis, Reading (title)
3rd Divisional Signals	J R Gaunt & Sons, Montreal

4th Canadian Division

38th Battalion	J R Gaunt & Sons, Birmingham
44th Battalion	J W Tiptaft & Son, Birmingham
46th Battalion	Service Supply, Rochester
47th Battalion	J W Tiptaft & Son, Birmingham
50th Battalion	Goldsmiths & Silversmiths, London (cap)
	J W Tiptaft & Son, Birmingham (collar & title)
54th Battalion	Jacoby Bros, Vancouver
	J W Tiptaft & Son, Birmingham (C/54)
72nd Battalion	Moore, Taggart & Co., Glasgow
	J W Tiptaft & Son, Birmingham (collar & title)
75th Battalion	J W Tiptaft & Son, Birmingham
	Savoy Tailors Guild, London (titles)
78th Battalion	J W Tiptaft & Son, Birmingham
85th Battalion	J W Tiptaft & Son, Birmingham
87th Battalion	United Service Supply, London
102nd Battalion	H Ford, London
124th Pioneer Battalion	J W Tiptaft & Son, Birmingham
10th Trench Mortar Battery	Wheeler & Co, London
11th Trench Mortar Battery	The Jewellers Co, Haslemere, Surrey
11th Machine Gun Company	Townshend, Birmingham*
12th Machine Gun Company	C A Hodgkinson, London*
16th Machine Gun Company	Townshend, Birmingham*

*Machine Gun Corps badges

Corps

Canadian Artillery	Marsh Bros, Birmingham
	A W Gamage, London
	Shirley Brooks, Woolwich
	Thomas White, Aldershot
	Strickland & Son, London
	Savoy Tailors Guild, London
Canadian Engineers	J R Gaunt & Sons, Montreal

Source: Statement of Badges of Canadian Units, August 1917, D-209-33.

Appendix 9

GENERAL ROUTINE ORDERS

QUARTERMASTER GENERAL'S BRANCH

4663—Badges and Titles authorized to be worn by Canadian Units in France.—The Badges and Titles authorized to be worn by Canadian units in France, as shown in the following list, will be supplied by A.O.D.

As regards Badges Forage Cap, every Canadian Infantry Battalion is allowed a special Cap Badge which should be demanded under the designation of the Battalion concerned, with the exception of the 13th and 42nd Canadian Infantry Battalions who wear a Scarlet Hackle in lieu of Cap Badge.

When doubt exists as to whether the Cap Badge at present worn by units is that authorized, information on this point should be obtained from the A.D.O.S. Canadian Corps before demands are submitted.

Indents may be sent in through Ordnance Officers concerned, and issue will be made as supplies become available.

List of Badges authorized to be worn by Canadian units in France

Badges, Forage Cap, with pin:-

   Royal Canadian Dragoons.
   Lord Strathcona's Horse (R.C.).
   Fort Garry Horse.
   Canadian Light Horse.
   Royal Canadian Horse Artillery.
   Canadian Artillery, as for R.F.A. but with "CANADA" instead of "UBIQUE" universal for
      Field and Garrison.
   Canadian Engineers.
   Canadian Army Service Corps.
   Canadian Army Medical Corps.
   Canadian Army Veterinary Corps.
   Canadian Ordnance Corps.
   Canadian Army Pay Corps.
   Canadian Postal Corps.
   Canadian Machine Gun Corps, as worn my English M.G. Corps.
   Canadian Corps Cyclist Battalion.
   Canadian Military Police.
   Royal Canadian Regiment.
   P.P.C.L.I.
   1st Canadian Mounted Rifles.
   2nd   "   "   "
   4th   "   "   "
   5th   "   "   "
   Other Canadian Infantry Battalions.
   Canadian Army Dental Corps.

Maple Leaf with pin, worn by all units for which special badges are not authorized.

Titles, shoulder (metal) with pin:-

    Canada.—Worn by all Units for which special badges are not authorized.

    R.C.H.A.—Royal Canadian Horse Artillery.

    C.F.A.—Canadian Field Artillery.

    C.G.A.—Canadian Garrison Artillery.R.C.R.

    R.C.R.—Royal Canadian Regiment.

    Western Cavalry— 5th Canadian Infantry Battalion.

    R.H.C.—13th and 42nd Canadian Infantry Battalions.

    R.M.R.—14th Canadian Infantry Battalion.

    Canadian Scottish—16th Canadian Infantry Battalion

    V.R.C.—24th Canadian Infantry Battalion.

    R.C.D.—Royal Canadian Dragoons.

    Strathcona's—Lord Strathcona's Horse.

    F.G.H.—Fort Garry Horse.

    C.L.H.—Canadian Light Horse.

Titles Worsted:-

    C.E.—Canadian Engineers. Blue letters on red patch.

    P.P.C.L.I.—Princess Patricia's Canadian Light Infantry. White letters on red ground.

Badges, Collar (metal) with pin:-

    Canadian Light Horse.

    Lord Strathcona's Horse.

    Royal Canadian Dragoons.

    Royal Canadian Regiment.

    P.P.C.L.I.

    __1__ **

    C.M.R.   1st Canadian Mounted Rifles.

    __2__ **

    C.M.R.   2nd Canadian Mounted Rifles.

    __4__ **

    C.M.R.   4th Canadian Mounted Rifles.

    __5__ **

    C.M.R.   5th Canadian Mounted Rifles.   **see Note

    C___   worn by all Canadian Infantry Battalions except R.C.R. and P.P.C.L.I.

    1 (etc)   To be the numeral corresponding to the Battalion number, Surmounted by "C".

    Grenades, with pin, worn by all Artillery and Engineer units.

    Maple Leaf, with pin, worn by all units for which special badges not authorized.

(4004/23 (Q.B.1), 1-8-18)

4798—Badges and Titles of Canadian Units in France.The following amendment is made to G.R.O. 4663:—

Badges, forage cap, with pin:-

After "Canadian Machine Gun Corps, as worn by English Machine Gun Corps."

Add "except that the word 'Canada' is inserted between the stocks of the crossed machine guns"

Badges, collar, metal, with pin:

Insert- after "Canadian Ordnance Corps:—

"Canadian Machine Gun Corps"   same as cap badge.

(4004/23 (Q.B.1), 17-8-18)

** It was decided by the Director of Ordnance Services OMFC 25 March 1918 to supply regimental design collar badges for the CMR Battalions instead of those authorized in GRO 4663 (C-33-43 (Vol 1), Vol 3298*)

Source: RG9IIIB.1, Vol 3782

Appendix 10
Badges Received by Canadian Ordnance Depot
from J W Tiptaft & Son
April 1918 to May 1919

Unit	Cap	Collars (Pairs)	Titles (Pairs)
Fort Garry Horse	1,000	1,000	700
Canadian Light Horse		2,100	
A Squadron	700	700	
B Squadron	700	700	
C Squadron	700	700	
Royal Canadian Regiment	6,000		2,000
Princess Patricia's Canadian			
Light Infantry	1,000	1,000	
1st Battalion	1,000	(C/1) 1,000	
3rd Battalion	2,000	(C/3) 2,000	
4th Battalion	2,000	(C/4) 2,000	
5th Battalion	2,000	(C/5) 1,000	
7th Battalion	2,000	(C/7) 3,000	
8th Battalion	2,000	(C/8) 2,000	
10th Battalion	2,000	(C/10) 2,000	
13th Battalion	1,000	(C/13) 2,000	
14th Battalion			1,500
15th Battalion	1,000	(C/15) 2,000	1,500
16th Battalion	1,000	(C/16) 1,000	
18th Battalion	1,000	(C/18) 1,000	
19th Battalion	2,000	(C/19) 2,000	
20th Battalion	2,000	(C/20) 2,000	
21st Battalion	1,000	(C/21) 2,000	
22nd Battalion	1,000	(C/22) 2,000	
24th Battalion		(C/24) 2,000	1,500
25th Battalion	2,000	(C/25) 2,000	
26th Battalion	1,000	(C/26) 3,000	
27th Battalion	1,000	(C/27) 2,000	
28th Battalion	3,000	(C/28) 2,000	
29th Battalion	1,000	(C/29) 2,000	
31st Battalion	1,000	(C/31) 1,000	
38th Battalion	2,000	(C/38) 2,500	
42nd Battalion	1,000	(C/42) 1,000	
43rd Battalion	1,000	(C/43) 2,000	
44th Battalion	1,000	(C/44) 1,000	

46th Battalion	2,000	(C/46) 2,000
47th Battalion	1,000	(C/47) 1,000
49th Battalion	3,000	(C/49) 2,000
50th Battalion	1,000	(C/50) 1,000
52nd Battalion	4,000	(C/52) 3,000
54th Battalion	1,000	(C/54) 2,000
58th Battalion	1,000	(C/58) 1,000
72nd Battalion	2,000	(C/72) 2,000
75th Battalion	1,000	(C/75) 2,000
78th Battalion	2,000	(C/78) 2,000
85th Battalion	1,000	(C/85) 2,000
87th Battalion	1,000	(C/87) 2,000
102nd Battalion		(C/102) 1,000
116th Battalion	1,000	(C/116) 1,000
1st Canadian Mounted Rifles Bn	1,000	2,000
2nd Canadian Mounted Rifles Bn	2,000	2,000
4th Canadian Mounted Rifles Bn	3,000	2,000
5th Canadian Mounted Rifles Bn	1,000	1,000
Canadian Artillery	20,000	
Canadian Engineers	12,820	7,500
Canadian Army Service Corps	6,000	5,000
Canadian Army Dental Corps	100	
Canadian Corps Cyclist Battalion	500	500
Canadian Machine Gun Corps	20,500	14,500
Canadian Military Police Corps	500	500
Canadian Army Veterinary Corps	*500	*
Canadian Postal Corps	100	
Canadian Army Medical Corps	5,000	
Canadian Army Pay Corps	2,000		4,000
Canadian Ordnance Corps	500	

*800 cap badges and 800 pairs of collars also shipped from J R Gaunt & Sons.

Source: Letters from J W Tiptaft & Son advising shipment, C-1013-33.

Appendix 11
Canadian Ordnance Depot Ashford
Stock of Special Cap, Collar and Shoulder Badges
As at 20 January 1919

Unit	Badges Cap	Badges Collars (Pairs)	Badges Shoulder Initials (Pairs)
Royal Canadian Dragoons	3,824	1,404	3,743
Lord Strathcona's Horse			
(Royal Canadians)	1,182		953
Fort Garry Horse		400	
Canadian Light Horse			
A Squadron	458	500	
B Squadron	456	450	
C Squadron	436	500	
Royal Canadian Regiment	6,006	344	2,000
		(right)	
		1,523	
		(left)	
Princess Patricia's Canadian			
Light Infantry	228		
1st Battalion	300	2,040	
2nd Battalion	100	1,880	
3rd Battalion	850	900	
4th Battalion	850	900	
5th Battalion	850	1,109	
7th Battalion	850	1,000	
8th Battalion	748	995	
10th Battalion	650	1,000	
13th Battalion	1,000	1,220	48
14th Battalion	150	264	
15th Battalion	150	1,355	
16th Battalion		1,045	
18th Battalion	300	550	
19th Battalion	600	750	
20th Battalion	600	400	
21st Battalion	600	450	
22nd Battalion	100	500	
24th Battalion	1	850	
25th Battalion	900	400	
26th Battalion	500	850	
27th Battalion	249	810	

28th Battalion	1,050	378	
29th Battalion	550	378	
31st Battalion	600	550	
38th Battalion	300	800	
42nd Battalion	1,000	50	
43rd Battalion		75	
44th Battalion	200	300	
46th Battalion	500	300	
47th Battalion	600	550	
49th Battalion	800		
50th Battalion	400	350	
52nd Battalion		400	
54th Battalion	100	600	
58th Battalion	2		
72nd Battalion	400	600	
75th Battalion		950	
78th Battalion	300	300	
85th Battalion	400	250	
87th Battalion	600	250	
102nd Battalion	200	750	
116th Battalion	-	-	
1st Canadian Mounted Rifles Bn		1,000	
2nd Canadian Mounted Rifles Bn		250	
4th Canadian Mounted Rifles Bn	800	250	
5th Canadian Mounted Rifles Bn	200		
Royal Canadian Horse Artillery Brigade	137		505
Canadian Artillery	3,552		
Canadian Field Artillery			5,155
Canadian Garrison Artillery			2,394
Canadian Engineers	9,558		
-Artillery and Engineer grenades		5,800	
Canadian Army Service Corps			14,538
Canadian Army Dental Corps	110		2,502
Canadian Corps Cyclist Battalion	2		
Canadian Machine Gun Corps	1,550		
Canadian Military Police Corps	250		
Canadian Army Veterinary Corps	500		
Canadian Postal Corps	275		
Canadian Army Medical Corps	1,570		
General Service Maple leaf	91,834	141,359	
CANADA Shoulder Titles			32,232

Source: B-4-3(Vol 2).

Appendix 12
Use of Badges by CEF Medical Units

Unit	Cap Badge	Collar Badge	
Training Depot	maple leaf	maple leaf	
No 1 Field Ambulance	Cross 85-7-1	unknown	officers
	unknown	unknown	other ranks
No 2 Field Ambulance	Cross 85-7-2C	Cross 85-7-2C	makeshift
	maple leaf	maple leaf	used in 1917
No 3 Field Ambulance	CAMC	CAMC	officers
	CAMC	maple leaf	other ranks
No 4 Field Ambulance	Cross 85-7-4	Cross 85-7-4	
No 5 Field Ambulance	maple leaf	maple leaf	
No 6 Field Ambulance	CAMC	CAMC	officers
	maple leaf	maple leaf	other ranks
No 7 Field Ambulance	maple leaf	maple leaf	
No 8 Field Ambulance	Cross 85-7-8	Cross 85-7-8	
	CAMC*	Cross 85-7-8*	officers*
	maple leaf*	Cross 85-7-8*	other ranks*
			*worn in France
No 9 Field Ambulance	maple leaf	maple leaf	
No 10 Field Ambulance	unknown	unknown	
No 11 Field Ambulance	CAMC	maple leaf	
No 12 Field Ambulance	unknown	unknown	
No 13 Field Ambulance	unknown	unknown	
No 14 Field Ambulance	CAMC	CAMC	officers
	maple leaf	maple leaf	other ranks
No 15 Field Ambulance	Cross 85-7-2B**	Cross 85-7-2B**	
	** incorrectly shown as No 2 Field Ambulance		

No 16 Field Ambulance	unknown	unknown	
No 1 Casualty Clearing Station	CAMC CAMC	CAMC maple leaf	officers other ranks
No 2 Casualty Clearing Station	CAMC	CAMC	
No 3 Casualty Clearing Station	CAMC maple leaf	CAMC maple leaf	officers other ranks
No 4 Casualty Clearing Station	CAMC	CAMC	
No 2 Stationary Hospital	maple leaf	maple leaf	
No 3 Stationary Hospital	CAMC maple leaf	CAMC maple leaf	officers other ranks
No 7 Stationary Hospital	maple leaf	maple leaf distinctive	rare badge
No 8 Stationary Hospital	Cross 85-3-8	Cross 85-3-8	
No 9 Stationary Hospital	Cross 85-3-9	Cross 85-3-9	
No 10 Stationary Hospital	unknown	unknown	
No 1 General Hospital	CAMC maple leaf	CAMC maple leaf	officers other Ranks
No 2 General Hospital	CAMC	CAMC	
No 3 General Hospital	CAMC	CAMC	
No 4 General Hospital	unknown	unknown	
No 5 General Hospital	CAMC	CAMC	
No 6 General Hospital	maple leaf	maple leaf	
No 7 General Hospital	unknown	unknown	
No 8 General Hospital	CAMC maple leaf	CAMC maple leaf	officers other ranks
No 9 to 14 General Hospitals	unknown	unknown	

| No 15 General Hospital | CAMC | CAMC |
| No 16 General Hospital | unknown | unknown |

Sources: Submissions to Historical Section, Canadian War Records Office, 1917, RG9IIID.1, Vols 4714-4716; Letters from OC of Medical Units, 1922, RG24, Vol 1735, DHS 3-11 (Vol 2); Letter from AMC Training Depot, RG24, Vol 4260, 47-3-23; Will R Bird collection.

Appendix 13
Forestry Depots and Reinforcing Units
Raised in Military Districts Nos 4, 5, 6 and 11

Military Districts Nos 4 and 5 (Quebec)
Forestry Company MD No 4[1]
   Nos 3 and 4 Forestry Companies[2]

Forestry Company MD No 5[3]

Military District No 6 (New Brunswick, Nova Scotia and PEI)
Forestry Company New Brunswick[1]
   1st Forestry Reinforcing Draft from MD No 6[4]
   No 2 New Brunswick Forestry Company[2]

Forestry Depot MD No 6[3]
   2nd Forestry Reinforcing Draft from MD No 6[4]
   No 2 Nova Scotia Forestry Depot[2]

Military District No 11 (British Columbia and Yukon)
Forestry Company MD No 11[1]
Forestry Depot MD No 11[3]
   Forestry Draft Southern British Columbia[2]
   Forestry Company, Vancouver, BC[2]
   Forestry Company, Victoria, BC[2]
   Forestry Draft, Kamloops, BC[2]
   Forestry Draft, Kelowna, BC[2]
   Revelstoke Forestry Company[2]

Notes and References

1. Authorized 8 January 1917, AG to GOC MD No 6, RG24, Vol 4566, 133-67-1; published in GO 48/1917.

2. Appointment of Officers and Lists of Officers on Militia Orders 1917.

3. Authorized by GO 74/1917.

4. Nominal Rolls shows recruited in New Brunswick.

Appendix 14

CANADIAN EXPEDITIONARY FORCE
ROUTINE ORDERS

Applicable to C.E.F. Services in Canada and to the Active Militia called out on Active Service.

HEADQUARTERS, OTTAWA

26th APRIL 1918

492 AUTHORIZED BADGES ONLY TO BE WORN BY DRAFTS PROCEEDING-OVERSEAS

Drafts proceeding overseas will wear only the authorized C.E.F. badges of the arm of the service to which they belong, as detailed in the appendix to Orders of this date.

It is to be distinctly understood that the wearing of special badges is not permitted except as laid down in General Instruction No. 150, issued with Militia Orders 369-371.

Reference H.Q. 96-11-70. D.E.O.S. 467.

APPENDIX

Appendix to Canadian Expeditionary Routine Order No. 492 of 26th April 1918

DESIGNATION AND DETAIL OF BADGES APPROVED FOR ISSUE TO UNITS OF C.E.F. IN CANADA.

ARTICLE:		DETAIL:
Badges, cap:		
R.C.A.	Universal	Bronze
Engineers		Gunmetal
Maple Leaf		Bronze
Badges, collar:		
Artillery	Small Grenade	Gunmetal
Engineers	Small Grenade	"
A.S.C.		"
Maple leaf		Bronze
Initials, shoulder:		
C.A.M.C.		Gunmetal
C.A.D.C.		"
C.A.S.C.		"
C.A.V.C.		"
C.E.		"
C.F.A.		"
C.G.A.		"
Signal		"

Titles, shoulder;	Depot Battalions	
1 D.B.W.O. Canada	Western Ontario	Gunmetal
1 D.B.C.O. Canada	Central Ontario	"
2 D.B.C.O. Canada		
1 D.B.2 C.O. Canada		
2 D.B.2 C.O. Canada		
1 D.B.E.O. Canada	Eastern Ontario	"
1 D.B.Q. Canada	Quebec	"
2 D.B.Q. Canada		
1 D.B.2 Q. Canada		
2 D.B.2 Q. Canada		
1 D.B.N.S. Canada	Nova Scotia	"
1 D.B.N.B. Canada	New Brunswick	"
1 D.B.M. Canada	Manitoba	"
1 D.B.S. Canada	Saskatchewan	"
1 D.B.A. Canada	Alberta	"
1 D.B.B.C. Canada	British Columbia	"
2 D.B.B.C. Canada		

Permanent Force.

Details of the Permanent Force will wear their own regimental badges.

Reference: H.Q. 96-11-70, D.E.O.S. 467.

CANADIAN EXPEDITIONARY FORCE
ROUTINE ORDERS

Applicable to C.E.F. Services in Canada and to the Active Militia called out on Active Service.

HEADQUARTERS, OTTAWA

9 MAY 1918

541 BADGES ONLY TO BE WORN BY DRAFTS PROCEEDING OVERSEAS

The Appendix to Routine Order 492, of April 26, is amended by adding:

Article	**Detail**
Badges, cap—After Maple Leaf insert 1st Tank Battalion Gun Metal	
Badges collar—After Maple Leaf add 1st Tank Battalion Gun Metal	
Initials, shoulder—After Signal add CANADA	
Titles, shoulder—After 1.D.B.E.O. CANADA add 2.D.B.E.O. CANADA	
After 2. D.B.2 Q. CANADA add 3.D.B.2 Q. CANADA	

(Reference H.Q. 96-11-70. D.E.O.S. 467)

Appendix 15
CEF Pipe Band Sporran Badges

Units	Description of Badge
Princess Patricia's Canadian Light Infantry	Babin 40-1 (white metal)
15th, 21st, 35th, 43rd, 77th, 85th, 134th, 154th, 174th, 179th, 185th, 193rd, 219th, 231st (drummers) Battalions	Regular battalion badge
16th, 72nd, 113rd*, 173rd, 231st (pipers), 241st (pipers) Battalions	Regular battalion badge in silver or silver plate
17th Battalion	Seaforth Highlanders badge
19th Battalion	91st Regiment Canadian Highlanders badge
67th Battalion	Special badge in white metal for pipers*
102nd Battalion	Babin 40-4, smaller than glengarry badge*
228th Battalion	Silver grenade
246th Battalion	78th Pictou Regiment 'Highlanders' badge
Canadian Forestry Corps	Cross 30-1-2 (smaller, in silver)*

Sources: Stewart, Charles H: *"Overseas": The Lineages and Insignia of The Canadian Expeditionary Force 1914-1919,* Toronto 1970; *Durand collection.

Appendix 16
Report on Badge Collection prepared by the
Canadian War Records Office
January 1918

During the past six months the collection of Regimental Badges has been doubled and brought to a stage beyond which there appears to be little distance to go. Practically all units in England and France, who possess an individual Badge are represented in this collection. It has been verified by correspondence that 55 of the remaining units have no special Badge. Steps are being taken to ascertain which of the other units wear an individual Badge, but it is believed that there will be comparatively few to add to our files.

Regarding the 258 Infantry Battalions, all are represented with the following exceptions - 3 Battalions that have not left Canada, 6 Battalions that have not as yet replied to our Circular Letters, 4 Battalions who were not able to supply us or from whom we had no reply to our Circular Letters, and therefore have ordered Badges from the makers.

The remaining Badges on file are those of Miscellaneous Units, Pioneers, Artillery, C.A.M.C., Cavalry, etc.

METHOD OF OBTAINING BADGES

Our Circular Letter HSC.28 is sent to the Officer Commanding the unit of which we desire a Badge. Or in event of the unit having been absorbed, an HSC.27 is sent to the Officer Commanding the unit in which the original unit has been absorbed. If a reply is not received within a reasonable space of time, a follow-up letter, HSC.30 is sent, suggesting that our previous letter be treated as urgent. When these letters fail to bring results, steps are taken to find the manufacturers of the Badges required and they are purchased.

In the majority of cases a prompt reply has been forthcoming from the unit circularized, with the result that comparatively few Badges have had to be purchased.

FILING

Badges are mounted on white cardboard, size 6 1/2 x 4 3/4, one unit to each card, the cards being kept in slotted boxes holding 50 cards each.

Each card is placed in a numbered slot, corresponding to index on lid of each box. Each box is lettered, and an index is kept which shows at a glance the contents of the box.

A card index is also kept which shows the number of Badges on file, in Original Set, Duplicate Set, or Surplus and also quotes the Authority of the Badge, if any.

SUMMARY OF BADGES ON FILE

Individual Badges.	Original Set.		1,778
" "	Duplicate Set.		1,095
" "	Surplus Set.		259
Miscellaneous Badges.			330
		Total	3,462

This includes Officers & Other Ranks - Cap, Collar, Shoulder Badges and Numerals.

Surplus Set obtained by units sending Badges after unduly long silence during which Badges have been purchased, also by units sending more than were required for two sets.

Miscellaneous Badges are Numerals, Maple Leaf Cap and collar Badges, "Canada" Shoulder Badges and odd Letters.

Units represented.	325
Units with no special Badge(verified).	55
Sets of Badges ordered from manufacturers.	4
Units not heard from.	6

Total Badges on file July 1st, 1917	1,724
Total Badges on file January 1st, 1918	3,452
INCREASE	1,728

Source: RG9IIID.1, Vol 4720, Folder 118A, File 25.

Appendix 17

Notes on Design of Badges

Symbols on Badges

The design of the badge of a CEF unit often symbolized one or more characteristics of the unit. These included the following for the unit:

- Affiliation with a Militia or British Army Regiment or Corps
- Provincial, Regional or Municipal origins
- Unit's particular origin, traditions or other characteristics
- Type of unit, eg, Cavalry, Infantry, Rifles, Pioneers, etc

The design of CEF badges often featured two symbols of Canada, the beaver and the maple leaf. The beaver was the earliest symbol. It appeared on the Arms granted in 1632 by Charles I to Sir William Alexander of Nova Scotia.[1] The fur trade was the major economic activity in the early French and British colonies. The beaver also appeared on the Arms of the Hudson's Bay Company granted by Charles II in 1670.[1] The earliest use of the beaver on a Canadian Militia badge was that introduced about 1866 for the Militia of the Province of Canada. The beaver is found on about sixteen percent of the CEF badges.

The early colonists in Eastern Canada found the forests abundant with maple trees. The maple leaf was a symbol used on banners during the dedication of Brock's monument in 1853 and during the visit of HRH The Prince of Wales at Toronto in 1860.[2] It was included in the Arms granted to the Provinces of Ontario and Quebec in 1868. In the 1870s, the maple leaf was used in the design of the badges of the 2nd Battalion 'Queen's Own Rifles of Toronto' and the 51st Battalion of Infantry 'Hemmingford Rangers'. About sixty percent of all CEF badges were either of the maple leaf design or featured the maple leaf. Another quarter of the badges included maple leaves in their design.

The badge designs for some French Canadian units included the fleur-de-lis. The fleur-de-lis appeared on the *Grand Bannière de France* which was in use when Jacques Cartier made his first voyage to Canada in 1534[3]. The fleur-de-lis appeared on the colours of three of the units of France that garrisoned Acadia and New France until 1760. The fleur-de-lis was included in the Arms granted to the Province Quebec in 1868. The first use of the fleur-de-lis in the design of a Canadian Militia badge was that of the 9th Battalion 'Voltigeurs de Quebec' authorized in March 1892.

Affiliation with a Militia or British Army Regiments or Corps

Following are the CEF units whose badge was either based on the design of the badge of their affiliated Canadian Militia Regiment or Corps or included symbols from their badge:

Infantry	*Symbol & Regiment*
8th, 90th, 144th, 190th, 203rd Battalions	Cap badge and 8th Bn collar badge design from the 90th Regiment 'Winnipeg Rifles' badge
6th Battalion	Fort Garry gate from the 34th 'Fort Garry Horse' badge
15th, 92nd, 134th Battalions	Badge design from the 48th Regiment 'Highlanders' badge[4]

17th Battalion	Stag's head from the 78th Pictou Regiment 'Highlanders' badge
24th Battalion	Maltese cross on 1st issue of badges from the 3rd Regiment 'Victoria Rifles of Canada' helmet plate; Cap badge (2nd issue) and officer's collar badge, badges of the Regiment
43rd, 174th, 179th, 14th Reserve Battalions	Badge design from The 79th Cameron Highlanders of Canada badge
55th Battalion	Moose from the 74th Regiment 'Brunswick Rangers' badge
72nd Battalion	Cap badge of The 72nd Seaforth Highlanders of Canada; stag's head on the collar badge from the Regiment's badge
75th Battalion	Unicorn's head gorged with coronet from the 9th Mississauga Horse badge
78th Battalion	Cap badge design from the 100th 'Winnipeg Grenadiers'
79th Battalion	Buffalo from the badge of the 12th Manitoba Dragoons[5]
83rd, 166th, 255th Battalions	Badge design from the 2nd Regiment 'Queen's Own Rifles of Canada' badge[6]
84th, 169th Battalions	Badge design from the 109th Regiment badge
87th, 245th Battalions	Cap badge of the 1st Regiment Canadian Grenadier Guards
88th Battalion	Grenade on ORs cap badge from the 88th Regiment Victoria Fusiliers ORs cap badge; ORs collar badge is the Regiment's ORs collar badge; Officer's badges are the Regiment's officer's badges
100th Battalion	Cap badge of the 100th 'Winnipeg Grenadiers'
107th Battalion	Wolf from the badge of the 32nd Manitoba Horse
121st Battalion	Grenade is the 11th Regiment Irish Fusilier of Canada badge
123rd Battalion	Star device is the 10th Regiment 'Royal Grenadiers' badge[7]
124th Battalion	Unicorn rampant gorged with coronet from the 9th Mississauga Horse badge
127th, 220th Battalions	Badge design from the 12th Regiment 'York Rangers' badge[8]
129th Battalion	Shield with the leopard's heads surmounted by gryphon from badge of the 77th Wentworth Regiment and Arms of the County of Wentworth, Ont[9]
130th Battalion	Badge design from the 42nd Lanark and Renfrew Regiment

139th Battalion	Badge design from the 40th Northumberland Regiment
158th Battalion	Shield bearing the Arms of The Duke of Connaught from the cap badge of the 6th Regiment, The Duke of Connaught's Own Rifles'
159th Battalion	The head of a bull moose from the 97th Regiment 'Algonquin Rifles' badge[10]
170th Battalion	Unicorn rampant gorged with coronet and motto is the badge of the 9th Mississauga Horse[11]
172nd Battalion	The head of a mountain sheep from the 102nd Regiment, Rocky Mountain Rangers badge
173rd Battalion	The device and motto is the 91st Regiment Canadian Highlanders badge[12]
186th Battalion	Badge design from the 24th 'Kent' Regiment badge
199th Battalion	1st issue of badge design from the 55th Regiment badge
208th Battalion	Harp from the 110th Irish Regiment badge
225th Battalion	Elk's head from the 107th East Kootenay badge
244th Battalion	The star of eight large and eight small points from the 3rd Regiment 'Victoria Rifles of Canada' cap badge
248th Battalion	The shield with the lion rampant and the lion and lioness supporters from the 31st Grey Regiment badge and the Arms of the County of Grey, Ont[13]
6th Regiment (D.C.O.R.) Overseas Draft	Monogram device is the 6th Regiment 'Duke of Connaught's Own Rifles' collar badge
11th Regiment (I.F.C.) Overseas Draft	Grenade is the 11th Regiment Irish Fusiliers of Canada badge
50th Regiment Overseas Draft	Stag's head erased from the 50th Regiment cap badge

Artillery

Canadian Siege and Field Artillery	Gun cap badge the Canadian Artillery badge

Mounted Rifles

Depot Regiment Canadian Mounted Rifles	Horse rampant from 1st Hussars collar badge; Brock's monument from 2nd Dragoons collar badge; horse's head from 4th Hussars badges[14]

Machine Gun Corps

9th MG Company, Yukon Motor MG Battery	Badge design from the Canadian Machine Gun Corps badge

Service Corps

No 1 ASC Training Depot,
    4th Divisional Train, ASP   Eight-pointed star from the Canadian Army
    Mechanical Transport Coy   Service Corps badge

Medical Service

Nos 4, 8 (title), 10 (title),   Maple wreath, crown and Rod of Aesculapius
    15 Field Ambulance   from CMC badge

No 9 Stationary Hospital   Rod of Aesculapius from CMC badge

Corps Cyclists

No 4 Divisional Cyclist   True and magnetic north points from the Corps
    Company   of Guides badge

Other Corps

Canadian Army Pay
    Corps CEF   Beaver from Canadian Army Pay Corps badge

Other CEF units based their badge on the design of their affiliated British Army Regiment or Corps or included symbols from the badge:

Infantry	*Symbol & Regiment*
13th Battalion	Badge design from The Black Watch (Royal Highland Regiment) badge
42nd Battalion	Cap badge of The Black Watch (Royal Highland Regiment); officer's collar badge design from their badge
73rd Battalion	Officer's collar badge design from The Black Watch (Royal Highland Regiment) collar badge
198th Battalion	The dragon on 2nd issue cap badge from The Buffs (East Kent) Regiment of Foot[15]; collar badges are that Regiment's collar badge[16]
231st Battalion	Cap badge of the Seaforth Highlanders (Ross-shire Buffs, The Duke of Albany's); stag's head and Duke of Albany's cypher on the collar badge from that Regiment's badge

Machine Gun Corps

Canadian MG Corps   Badge design from the British MG Corps badge

Medical Service

Canadian Medical Corps   Badge design from the Royal Army Medical
    CEF   Corps badge

Chaplain Service

| Canadian Chaplains CEF | Maltese cross badge from British Army Chaplains badge |

Military Police

| Military Police CEF | Badge design (1st issue) from the Corps of Military Police of the British Army badges |

Corps Cyclists

| Canadian Corps Cyclist Battalion, Reserve Cyclist Company | Badge design from the British Army Cyclist Corps badge[17] |

Provincial, Regional or Municipal Origins

Some units indicated their Provincial origin by including on their badge the Arms or part of the Arms of their Province:

Infantry	*Symbol*
22nd, 69th, 258th Battalions	Arms of the Province of Quebec
25th Battalion	Shield from the ancient Arms of the Colony of Nova Scotia
31st, 50th, 82nd, 89th Battalions	Arms of the Province of Alberta
45th Battalion	Arms of the Province of Manitoba
46th, 65th, 188th, 217th Battalions	Arms of the Province of Saskatchewan
85th, 106th, 112th, 185th, 193rd, 219th, 246th Battalions	Arms of the Province of Nova Scotia[18]
93rd, 161st Battalions	Shield from the Arms of the Province of Ontario
104th, 115th, 140th, 145th Battalions,	Arms of the Province of New Brunswick
105th Battalion	Shield from the Arms of the Province of Prince Edward Island
184th Battalion	Buffalo from the Arms of the Province of Manitoba[44]
1st Depot Bn NS Regiment	Arms of the Province of Nova Scotia[18]
Depot Bns 1st & 2nd Quebec Regiments	Arms of the Province of Quebec
1st Depot Battalion Manitoba Regiment	Arms of the Province of Manitoba
1st Depot Battalion Alberta Regiment	Arms of the Province of Alberta

1st & 2nd Depot Bns B C Regiment	Arms of the Province of British Columbia

Artillery

No 9 Depot Battery Siege Artillery	Arms of the Province of New Brunswick

No 5 Siege Artillery
    Draft
	Oak trees on an island from the Arms of the Province of
	    Prince Edward Island

King's County Siege
    Artillery Draft
	Oak trees on an island from the Arms of the Province of
	    Prince Edward Island

Pioneers

3rd Pioneer Battalion	Arms of the Province of British Columbia

Machine Gun Corps

NB MG Draft	Arms of the Province of New Brunswick

Forestry Corps

Les Forestiers de Quebec	Arms of the Province of Quebec

Some battalions included the Arms or part of the Arms of their City, Town or County of origin:

Infantry	*Symbol*
23rd Battalion	Arms of the City of Montreal
27th Battalion	Arms of the City of Winnipeg

129th Battalion	Shield with the leopard's heads surmounted by gryphon
	    from the Arms of the County of Wentworth, Ont and
	    the badge of the 77th Wentworth Regiment[9]

142nd Battalion	Arms of the City of London, Ont[19]
149th Battalion	Ram's head from the Arms of the County of Lambton, Ont
152nd Battalion	Arms of the City of Weyburn[20]
171st Battalion	Shield of Quebec City[21]
186th Battalion	Arms of the County of Kent, Ontario from the badge of the 24th 'Kent' Regiment
191st Battalion	Arms of the Town of Macleod, Alta[22]
195th Battalion	Crest from the Arms of the City of Regina[23]

248th Battalion	The shield with the lion rampant and the lion and
	    lioness supporters from the Arms of the County of
	    Grey, Ont and the 31st Grey Regiment badge[13]

Artillery
No 10 Depot Battery
   Siege Artillery   Arms of the City of Halifax[24]

Other battalions indicated their Regional origins by including depictions of animals that inhabit the Region:

Infantry	*Animals*
49th Battalion	Face of a coyote, the mascot of the battalion[25]
55th, 128th, 141st, 159th Battalions	Head of a moose
67th Battalion	Head of a wild cat
79th, 233rd, 243rd[26] Battalions	Buffalo
103rd Battalion	Head of a timber wolf
125th Battalion	Bear, for the Six Nation Indians[27]
163rd Battalion	Porcupine[28]
181st, Battalion	Bobcat after the team from Brandon College called the "Bobcats"
187th Battalion	Head of a Deer, denoting the Bn HQ at Red Deer[29]
214th Battalion	Wild cat
226th Battalion	Grizzly bear
228th Battalion	Head of a polar bear

Mounted Rifles	
1st CMR	Head of a buffalo
4th, 6th, 10th CMRs	Head of a moose

Other units included a variety of symbols on their badge to represent their Region of origin:

Infantry	*Symbol*
44th, 68th, 181st, 209th, 229th Battalions	Wheat sheaf or wheat sheaves
122nd Battalion	Muskoka logging scene
162nd Battalion	Tree stump and crossed axes, denoting logging in the Parry Sound District
175th Battalion	Stetson Hat, the symbol of Medicine Hat
176th Battalion	Horse Shoe Falls, Niagara Falls, Ont
188th Battalion	Axes and log, representing the lumber industry in Northern Saskatchewan[30]
Yukon Infantry Detachment	Collar badge was a miner's pan with a few grains of gold

Machine Gun Corps
Yukon Motor MG Battery   Miner's pan

Unit Origin, Traditions or Other Characteristics

Some battalions were raised from a particular ethnic group, men from particular group or followed a particular tradition, eg a Scottish Regiment. Various symbols appeared on the badges to denote these origins or traditions:

Infantry	*Symbol*	*Denotes*
16th, 96th Battalions	St. Andrew's cross	A Scottish Battalion
41st, 57th, 230th, 233rd Battalions	Fleur-de-lis	Bataillons Canadien Français
96th Battalion	Scottish Lion rampant (collar badges)	A Scottish Battalion
97th, 211th, 212th, 213th, 237th Battalions	Arms of George Washington	Personnel recruited from former American citizens
114th Battalion	Crossed tomahawks	A compliment to members of the Six Nations in the Battalion[31]
143rd, 216th Battalions	Bantam cock	A Bantam Battalion (height of ORs did not exceed 5' 2")
85th, 154th, 185th, 193rd, 194th, 219th, 246th Battalions	Thistles	Scottish Battalions
165th Battalion	Five pointed star	Star from the Acadian flag[32]
197th Battalion	Viking Ship	A Scandinavian Battalion
199th, 208th Battalions	Shamrock(s)	Irish Battalions
218th Battalion	Harp (badges), Shamrocks (shoulder title)	An Irish Battalion
223rd Battalion	Viking warrior crossed oars & battle axe	Most personnel of Scandinavian origin[33]
236th Battalion	St Andrew & Cross	A Scottish Battalion
241st Battalion	Scottish Lion's Head	A Scottish Battalion
10th Reserve Bn	Fleur-de-lis	Bataillon Canadien Français
No 1 Jewish Infantry Company	Star of David	A Jewish unit

Some units were raised or sponsored by Universities. Their badge design included the Arms or part of the Arms of the University:

Infantry	Symbol	Denotes
148th Battalion	Martlet	From the Arms of McGill University which sponsored the raising of the Battalion
196th Battalion	Arms of Universities of BC, Alta, Sask, Man	Battalion raised from these Universities
253rd Battalion	Arms of Queen's University	Recruited from graduates of the University
University of Toronto Overseas Training Company	Arms of University of Toronto	Recruited at the University

Artillery		
No 6 Battery Siege Artillery	Arms of McGill University	Recruited at the University
McGill Overseas Siege Artillery Draft	Arms of McGill University	Recruited at the University
67th Depot Battery	Arms of University of Toronto	Recruited at the University

Medical Service		
No 15 Field Ambulance	Arms of Queen's University	Recruited under the patronage of the University[34]
No 7 Stationary Hospital	Elements of the Arms of Dalhousie University	Recruited at the University
No 8 Stationary Hospital	Arms of University of Saskatchewan	Recruited at the University

Type of Unit

Some units had symbols on their badges denoting the type of unit or the type of units that contributed to its formation. These were:

Infantry	Symbol	Denotes
5th Battalion	Horse rampant	Formed from Cavalry Regiments
11th Battalion	Grenade & bugle	Formed from Fusilier, Grenadier and Rifle Regiments[35]
32nd Battalion	Horseshoe	Formed from Cavalry Regiments[36]
63rd, 163rd, 150th, 171st, 202nd, 234th Battalions	Crossed rifles	
103rd Battalion	Horseshoes	Raised by a Cavalry Unit

106th Battalion	Rifles with fixed bayonet	
259th, 260th Battalions	Bugle Horn	

Cavalry

8th Regiment CMR	Spurs	
Remount Depot	Horse's head	Formed from Cavalry Regiments

Artillery

10th, 11th Trench Mortar Batteries	Trench mortar	
10th Trench Mortar Battery (2nd issue)	Two ancient mortars & grenade	

Pioneers

1st Pioneer Battalion	Crossed pick & shovel	
2nd Pioneer Battalion	Crossed axes & grenade	Grenade represented Engineers in the Battalion[37]
4th Pioneer Battalion	Crossed pick & rifle	
Pioneer Drafts	Crossed pick & shovel	
Pioneer Training Depot	Wheel, crossed pick & rifle	

Machine Gun Corps

3rd MG Company	Vickers MG	
4th MG Company	Front of Vickers MG	
1st Motor MG Brigade	Automobile wheel & Colt MG	
Borden's MG Battery	Armoured Car	

Corps Cyclists

No 1, No 2 Divisional Cyclist Companies	Cycle Wheel	
No 3 Divisional Cyclist Company, Cyclist Drafts	Winged wheel	

Forestry Corps

Canadian Forestry Corps	Forest scene & stag	
224th, 238th, 242nd Battalions	Crossed axes	
230th, 238th Battalions	Tree or trees	

12th, 50th, 70th Forestry Companies	Crossed axes, trees
NB, NS Forestry Units	Crossed axes or tree
Winnipeg Forestry Company	Forest scene & crossed axes

Railway Troops

Overseas Railway Construction Corps	Locomotive driving wheel	
239th Railway Construction Bn, 3rd Battalion CRT	Locomotive driving wheel	
256th Railway Construction Bn, 10th Battalion CRT	Railway tracks & tunnel	
257th Railway Construction Bn,	Locomotive, crane & tracks	
No 1 Construction Battalion	Crossed shovel & sledge-hammer, pick axe handle	
No 2 Construction Battalion	Bridge supported by two trestles	
6th Battalion CRT	Grenade	Originally 228th Battalion (Northern Fusiliers)
Nos 1, 2, 3 Sections Skilled Railway Employees	Front of a locomotive	
Canadian Railway Troops Depot	Locomotive driving wheel, crossed platelayer's hammer & rifle	

Tank Corps

Canadian Tank Corps	Tank
1st, 2nd, 3rd Tank Battalions	Tank

Other Symbols

A variety of other symbols appeared on badges. Some were British symbols, eg the lion, bulldog, Union flag, which reflected the very close ties of the time with the United Kingdom and the British Empire. The significance of some of the other symbols were determined from the CEF records, or were obvious, but for some others, their meaning has been lost.

Infantry	Symbol	Denotes
29th Battalion (Officer's cap badge)	A winged rod entwined with serpents on a shield	
49th Battalion	Windmill	Flanders, where the unit had its first engagement[25]
101st Battalion	Lion's face	
102nd Battalion	Indian head and head-dress	
108th Battalion	Game cock	The Red Feather Poultry Farm which was turned into Barracks for the Battalion[38]
111th Battalion	Thistle	Scottish origins of the Town of Galt
125th Battalion	Oak log & pine log bound together	The Treaties binding the Six Nations Indians and the British[27]
160th Battalion	Thistle (collar badge)	Scottish origins of Bruce County
165th, 247th Battalions	Union flags	
192nd Battalion	Lion sitting	"an allusion to the name of Lieut-Col Lyon"[39] (OC of the Battalion)
199th Battalion	Monogram	Monogram of HRH Duchess of Connaught
200th Battalion	Lion cubs rampant	Overseas troops referred to in the UK as "Lions Cubs"[40]
205th Battalion	Tiger's face	
206th, 222nd Battalions	Lion rampant	
210th Battalion	Badge of the Legion of Frontiersmen[41]	
215th Battalion	Gryphon	From the family crest of the Cockshutt family[42]
221st Battalion	Bulldog standing[43]	
232nd Battalion	Lion on the trail	
235th Battalion	Lion sitting	
250th Battalion	Eagle	
University Overseas Companies	Open book	
Artillery		
79th Depot Battery	Grenade	
Mounted Rifles		
2nd Brigade CMR	Lion standing	

Labour Group
4th Labour Battalion   Demi-man, naked holding a club

Railway Troops
3rd, 4th, 11th, 12th
     Battalions CRT   Corps patch with a brass centre

Other Corps or Units
Canadian Army Dental
     Corps   Arch & pillars
Khaki University   Open book

Notes and References

1. Stanley, George F C, *The Story of Canada's Flag*, Toronto, 1965, p. 21.
2. *ibid*, p.23.
3. *ibid*, p.12.
4. CO 48th Regiment 'Highlanders' to OC 92nd Battalion, 6 December 1915 granted permission to use the badge and motto of the Regiment on the battalion badge, RG24, Vol 1536, 683-110-2; CO 48th Regiment 'Highlanders' to OC 134th Battalion, 24 December 1915 granted permission to use the badge and designation of the Regiment, RG24, Vol 1542, 683-177-3.
5. OC 79th Battalion to Canadian War Records Office, 22 November 1916 states that "...the Buffalo, which is essentially Western, and which is the badge of the 12th Manitoba Dragoons ... to which I, as OC of the 79th Battalion belong", RG9IIID.1, Vol 4698, Folder 65, File 2.
6. OC 166th Battalion to AAG 2nd Division, 4 February 1916 contains approval of the OC 2nd Regiment 'Queen's Own Rifles of Canada' to use the badge of the Regiment for the badge of the 83rd and 166th Battalions, RG24, Vol 4347, 34-4-7 (vol 2).
7. OC 123rd Battalion to Canadian War Records Office, 20 November 1916, RG9IIID.1, Vol 4700, Folder 71, File 8.
8. CO 12th Regiment 'York Rangers' to OC 220th Battalion, 26 February 1916 grants permission to use the badge of the Regiment for the badge of the 127th and 220th Battalions, RG24, Vol 1649, 683-290-1.
9. DCO MD No 2 to The Secretary, Militia Council, 19 April 1916, RG24, Vol 4347, 34-4-7 (vol 3).
10. OC 97th Regiment 'Algonquin Rifles' to OC 159th Battalion, 11 May 1917 granted permission to use the bull moose and wording "1st Algonquins" on the 159th Battalion badge, RG24, Vol 1639, 683-269-2.
11. GOC 2nd Division to The Secretary, Militia Council, 18 February 1916, RG24, Vol 1547, 683-249-1.
12. CO 91st Regiment 'Canadian Highlanders' to OC 173rd Battalion, 7 February 1916, RG24, Vol 1548, 683-258-1.
13. CO 31st Grey Regiment to OC 248th Battalion, 11 April 1915 granted permission to use the badge of the Regiment on the battalion badge, RG24, Vol 4348, 34-4-7 (vol 5).
14. OC Depot Regiment Canadian Mounted Rifles to DAA & QMG MD No 2, 22 May 1916 states that OCs of the 1st Hussars, 2nd Dragoons and 4th Hussars granted permission to use the crest of the regiments in the design of their badge, RG24, Vol 4347, 34-4-7 (vol 3).
15. HRH The Governor General stated in Dispatch No 629, 16 June 1916 that HM The King approved the Battalion to wear the badge of The Buffs (East Kent Regiment), RG24, Vol

1650, 683-292-2.

16. Approved 25 June 1917, AG Canadians to HQ Canadian Troops, Witley, RG9IIIB.1, Vol 2688, B-72-33.

17. ADOS Canadian Corps to DOS, 18 December 1917, RG9IIIB.1, Vol 884, B-4-3 (Vol 2).

18. These Arms were granted to the Province of Nova Scotia 26 May 1868 and superseded by their present Arms on 19 January 1929.

19. AO 1st Divisional Area to The Secretary, Militia Council, 14 January 1916, RG24, Vol 4260, 47-3-10.

20. OC 152nd Battalion to AAG i/c Administration MD No 10, 10 May 1916, RG24, Vol 1667, 683-332-1.

21. QM 171st Battalion to Canadian War Records Office, 23 May 1917, RG9IIID.1, Vol 4702, Folder 76, File 4.

22. Secretary-Treasurer Town of Macleod to OC 191st Battalion, 16 May 1916, granted permission to use the Arms of the Town on badges, RG24, Vol 1682, 683-369-1.

23. Mayor City of Regina to Minister of Militia, 8 March 1916, granted permission to use the Arms of the City on 195th Battalion badges. RG24, Vol 1652, 683-297-1.

24. OC No 10 Siege Battery to DAA&QMG MD No 6, 24 November 1916, RG24, Vol 1714, 683-480-1.

25. OC 49th Battalion to Canadian War Records Office, 21 May 1917, RG9IIID.1, Vol 4696, Folder 60, File 2 describes the head as that of as a wolf. It was that of a coyote, the Battalion mascot given at Lestock, Saskatchewan while on its way east to embark for overseas.

26. OC 243rd Battalion to OC 15 Canadian Reserve Battalion, 18 June 1917 stated that the "battalion was recruited from the plains and prairies of Saskatchewan, whereon the buffalo roamed in the early days of the West, RG9IIID.1, Vol 4705, Folder 82, File 22.

27. GOC 2nd Division to The Secretary, Militia Council, 18 February 1918, RG24, Vol 1548, 683-259-1.

28. OC 163rd Battalion to QMG, 12 January 1916, RG24, Vol 1546, 683-229-1, referring to the porcupine, states that the motto translated is "he who rubs against it gets stung".

29. Capt 187th Battalion to OC 21st Reserve Battalion, 31 May 1917, RG9IIID.1, Vol 4702, Folder 77, File 17.

30. Capt 188th Battalion to Canadian War Records Office, 22 March 1917, RG9IIID.1, Vol 4702, Folder 77, File 20.

31. OC 114th Battalion to Canadian War Records Office, 23 May 1917, RG9IIID.1, Vol 4699, Folder 70, File 5.

32. OC MD No 6 to The Secretary, Militia Council, 6 May 1916 RG24, Vol 1662, 683-316-1

33. OC 223rd Battalion to Canadian War Records Office, 15 July 1917, RG9IIID.1, Vol 4704, Folder 81, File 7.

34. OC No 15 Field Ambulance to Canadian War Records Office, 16 April 1917, RG9IIID.1, Vol 4715, Folder 108, File 4.

35. OC 11th Reserve Battalion to Commander 4th Canadian Training Brigade, 11 August 1916, RG9IIID.1, Vol 4691, Folder 49, File 16.

36. OC 32nd Battalion to Canadian War Records Office, 20 November 1916, RG9IIID.1, Vol 4694, Folder 56, File 11.

37. OC 2nd Pioneer Battalion to Canadian War Records Office, 16 May 1917, RG9IIID.1, Vol 4709, Folder 92, File 6.

38. OC 108th Battalion to Canadian War Records Office, 12 March 1917, RG9IIID.1, Vol 4699, Folder 69, File 7.

39. OC 192nd Battalion to Canadian War Records Office, 15 December 1916, RG9IIID.1, Vol 4703, Folder 78, File 7.

40. OC 200th Battalion to AAG i/c Administration MD No 10, 4 April 1916, RG24, Vol 1653,

683-298-1.

41. Acting Chief Executive Officer, Legion of Frontiersmen to Militia HQ, 24 March 1917 stated that this badge was used by the Battalion without their approval, RG24, Vol 1688, 683-388-1.

42. GOC 2nd Division to The Secretary Militia Council, 7 March 1916, RG24, Vol 4347, 34-4-7 (vol 2).

43. The bulldog standing is found on the badge of the 18th Mounted Rifles. However, no connection has been found between the 18th Mounted Rifles and the 221st Battalion.

44. OC 11th Canadian Reserve Battalion to the Canadian War Records Office, 25 June 1917, RG9IIID.1, Vol 4702, Folder 77, File 11.

Notes and References

Chapter 1: Policies and Practices for Badges

1. For illustration see Mazeas MS.5.

2. MO 539, 30 November 1914, *Canadian Priced List of Stores, Clothing and Necessaries - Part 1, 1912 Amendments* and MO 164, 29 March 1915, *Canadian Expeditionary Force - Clothing and Equipment*. This cancelled and replaced MO 524, 23 November 1914 as amended by MO 11, 4 January 1915; QMG Canadian Militia to OC Divisions and Districts, 12 January 1915, RG24, Vol 1507, 683-2-1.

3. Provincial Archives of Alberta, Photographs A5528-29, First Edmonton Detachment going overseas 1914, shows men at the railway station, some in uniform and some in civilian clothes; Bone, *Alberta Units*, pp.13-14 , states that an officer who went overseas with the 9th Battalion advised that when the battalion was formed they wore the badges of the 101st Regiment 'Edmonton Fusiliers' and continued to wear them until mid 1915; Glenbow Archives, Panorama photograph PE 77-1, 10th Battalion at Valcartier 1914 shows a small number wearing a variety of badges, but most do not have any badges.

4. CO 2nd Battalion Edmonton Regiment to HQ MD No 13, not dated [c1921], DHH Files. NAC Photograph PA-491 of the 9th Battalion after church parade at Plymouth, October 1914 shows the unit wearing the General Service maple leaf cap badges.

5. RG9IIIC.3, Vol 4045, Folder 2, File 3.

6. OC 12th Reserve Battalion to HQ 7th Infantry Brigade re Account of Hicks & Sons, 14 October 1915, 4-2-18.

7. RG9IIIB.1, Vol 381, A-85-1.

8. *ibid,* Vol 861, U-18-2.

9. *ibid,* Vol 861, 4-2-18, Carson to Secretary War Office, 16 February 1916.

10. Battalion Order 550, 18 June 1916, refers to "the new cap badge", RG9IIIC.3, Vol 4073, folder 10.

11. The numerals are professionally brazed on the General Service maple leaf cap badge which is marked "P W Ellis Co 1914". However, Glenbow Archives, photographs NA 4026-16, Ernest H. Marles, September 1915 and NA-4732-1 Sgt A W Bennett, November 1915 shows both wearing a General Service maple leaf cap badge without numerals and C over 10 collar badges.

12. Cross refers to these as "Interim Issues"; Cross 41B, 85C, 90B, 99B, 135B, 136B, 142B, 149C, 157C, 168C, 177D, 235C.

13. Glenbow Archives photo ND 3-79, Officers of the 49th Battalion, April 1915, shows the Officers wearing the same makeshift badge. City of Edmonton Archives, Panorama photograph EA10-293, 49th Battalion at the Exhibition Grounds, Edmonton 1915, shows only the Officers wearing this cap badge. The Other Ranks are wearing the General Service maple leaf cap badge without a numeral below.

14. DAA & QMG 2nd Division to Battalions being raised, 8 September 1915 and to OC 215th Battalion, 26 February 1916, 34-4-7 (Vols 1 & 2).

15. Harker, Douglas E. *The Dukes, the Story of the Men who served in Peace and War with the British Columbia Regiment (D.C.O.). 1883-1973,* picture of Officers of the 7th Battalion p.85.

16. 4-2-18.

17. Letter 18 February 1916, RG9IIIC.1, Vol 3876, Folder 6, File 1

18. RG24, Vol 6403, 96-11-59.

19. B-4-3.

20. Confirmation of order given to Elkington Co. 3 March 1915, for an additional 500 sets C over numeral for each of the 1st, 2nd, 3rd, 4th, 5th, 7th, 8th, 10th, 13th, 14th, 15th, 16th Battalions

to be shipped to AAA & QMG 1st Canadian Division, France, 4-2-18.

21. Hemsley to Carson, 28 March 1916 cites letter 26 March 1916 from HQ Aldershot Command; GOC 4th Canadian Division, Bramshott to HQ CEF, 22 June 1916, 4-2-18.

22. *Statement Regarding Badges to Canadian Units,* Byng to HQ Second Army, 16 August 1916, 4-2-18.

23. *Minutes of the Militia Council,* 96-11-70 (Vol 2)

24. Letter to HQ 7th Canadian Infantry Brigade, 10 February 1917, B-4-3.

25. *ibid,* 2 February 1917, B-4-3.

26. Letter to HQ 12th Canadian Infantry Brigade, 8 February 1917, B-4-3.

27. It is known that the City of Winnipeg donated the badges to the 27th Battalion. These were presented to the Battalion by the Mayor on 14 April 1916. (*Manitoba Free Press,* 14 April 1915; OC 27th Bn to Canadian War Records Office, 9 September 1916, RG9IIID.1, Vol 4693, Folder 54, File 13) Mrs J C Eaton donated the badges to Eaton's Machine Gun Battery (OC 2nd Division to Secretary Militia Council, 4 March 1915, 34-4-7 (vol 1)). However in most cases governments and individuals made cash gifts to the Battalion funds from which the badges were purchased.

28. RG9IIIC.3, Vol 4083, Folder 2, File 6.

29. Cited in Director of Ordnance Services to Deputy Minister OMFC, 30 April 1917, C-23-43 (Vol 2).

30. 96-11-70 (Vol 1).

31. Replies to Canadian Corps "Q" to requests for information on badges in use from: 1st Canadian Division, 29 August 1917; 2nd Canadian Division, 30 August 1917; 3rd Canadian Division, 31 August 1917; 4th Canadian Division, 27 August 1917, D-209-33.

32. ADOS 4/1, C-23-43 (Vol 1); B-4-3.

33. However extant uniforms of the 25th, 78th, 85th, 102nd Battalions show instances where the battalion collar badges were worn instead of the C over numeral, Glenbow Museum, Provincial Museum of Alberta, Victor Taboika Elbow War Museum.

34. Uniforms and photographs show Officers of the battalions wearing the battalion pattern collar badges. The 22nd Battalion Officers are seen wearing C over 22 however.

35. C-23-43 (Vol 2).

36. B-4-3 (vol 2).

Chapter 2: Reinforcing Unit Badges

c1 to c15. These references are to the table of Cross' catalogue numbers at the end of the Chapter.

1. 48th Highlanders Regimental Museum stated that the Company Sergeant-Major used the company funds to have the badge made in London, England after the company had been absorbed.

2. News Release *The Edmonton Journal,* 17 September 1915.

3. Bone, *Manitoba Units,* p.35.

4. Mazeas MM.224.

5. GOC MD No 10 to Secretary Militia Council, RG24, Vol 1547, 593-12-2.

6. The Loyal Scandinavian Draft was advised 13 September 1917 to wear the maple leaf badges, RG24, Vol 1730, 683-531-2.

7. Adjutant General Canadian Militia to OC Military Districts, 18 January 1917, RG24, Vol 4397, 34-7-193 (Vol 1).

8. This requirement was made clear a year later in CEF (Canada) ROs 492 and 682, 26 April 1918 and 17 June 1918 respectively.

9. CRO 271 Reorganization - Canadian Infantry Battalions, 20 January 1917. Published in MO 89 *Organization of Infantry Reserves of the CEF in England into Territorial Reserve Battalions and Regiments connected with Linked Battalions Overseas and with Recruiting*

Areas in Canada, 27 March 1917.

10. See Appendix 5 for details.

11. CEF (Canada) RO 492, 26 April 1918; Adjutant General's Branch, Internal Memo, 25 April 1918, RG24, Vol 1778, 683-670-4; Internal Memo MD No 2, 22 March 1918 states that 1st and 2nd Depot Battalions 1st Central Ontario Regiment and 1st Depot Battalion 2nd Central Ontario Regiment were wearing general issue maple leaf badges, 34-4-7 (Vol 5).

12. Militia Council Decision 1354, 10 December 1917; Adjutant General Canadian Militia Circular Letter 340, 12 December 1917, RG24, Vol 4555, 126-6-3-5; General Instruction 148, 31 December 1917.

13. Internal Memo Adjutant General's Branch, 25 April 1918, *op. cit.*, refers to approval on 683-705-2, but the file is missing.

14. Bone, *More Notes on Western Canadian Military Badges*, picture of 1st Depot Battalion Manitoba Regiment collar badge from the the collection of the late Charles B Hill-Tout.

15. These are known to have had sweetheart pins: 1st Depot Battalion New Brunswick Regiment, 1st Depot Battalion 1st Central Ontario Regiment, 1st Depot Battalion 2nd Central Ontario Regiment, 2nd Depot Battalion 2nd Central Ontario Regiment, 1st Depot Battalion Western Ontario Regiment, 1st Depot Battalion Saskatchewan Regiment.

16. C-23-43 (Vol 2).

17. Director of Ordnance Services to GOC Canadian Troops, Bramshott, 12 March 1917, C-23-43 (Vol 2).

18. Voucher sent 29 January 1917, RG9IIIB.1, Vol 1512, R-18-17.

19. RG9IIIC.13, Vol 4597, Folder 1, File 3.

20. OC 23rd Reserve Battalion to OC 10th Reserve Battalion, 20th February 1917, RG9IIIC.13, Vol 4597, Folder 1, File 3; OC 8th Reserve Battalion to Canadian War Records Office, RG9IIID.1, Vol 4707, Folder 89, File 13.

21. RG9IIID.1, Vol 4707, Folder 89, Files 4 & 11; Vol 4708 4708, Folder 90, Files 10 & 19.

22. *ibid*, Vol 4708, Folder 89, File 20; Vol 4691, Folder 49, File 16.

23. OC 9th Reserve Battalion to Historical Section, Canadian War Records Office, 19 May 1917, *ibid*, Vol 4691, Folder 49, File 2. When the 9th Battalion cap badge was made and worn remains a mystery. It is not recorded in the Inventory of the Canadian War Records Office Collection assembled in 1917-1918 when it was transferred to the Historical Section of the Army after the war. However, the Historical Section described the 9th Battalion cap badge in letter to James Davidson, Hamilton on 21 Sept 1921! It also did not appear on the Inventory of the Collection when it was transferred to the Dominion Archives in January 1929. Part of the die for the device on the maple leaf is in the Loyal Edmonton Regiment Museum.

24. *ibid*. Also contains an earlier letter to the Canadian War Records Office from OC 9th Reserve Battalion, 19th August 1916 stating that "up to the present there has not been a badge authorized for this unit."

25. *ibid*, Vol 4707, Folder 89, File 13.

26. It is known these had sweetheart pins: 4th, 12th, 15th, 20th, 24th, 25th, Reserve Battalions.

Chapter 3: Artillery Badges

c1 to c26. These references are to the table of Cross' catalogue numbers at the end of the Chapter.

1. Letter from OC RCHA Brigade, 29 June 1917, RG9IIID.1, Vol 4684, Folder 27, File 28.

2. GO 14/1918 and CEF (Canada) RO 492, 26 April 1918.

3. Babin 12-14, Cross 145-1-1.

4. For example the 43rd Battery purchased cap and shoulder badges. Toronto Stamp & Stencil Works Ltd, Invoice 19 January 1916, RG24, Vol 4260, 47-3-14.

5. Internal memo M D No 2, 27 October 1917, 34-4-47 (Vol 5).

6. 8th Battery CFA cap badge is the numeral '8' mounted on the wheel hub of Canada gun with wreath of maple leaves (McHugh, Type B) cap badge, Jeffrey Hoare, Sale 59, June 1998, Item 1544; 15th Battery CFA cap badge is a 79th Battery CFA cap badge (Cross 145-3-79A) with the numeral '7' filed down to be the numeral '1', Canadian War Museum Catalogue No 41-12-15-1-1; 36th Battery CFA cap badge is the shoulder numeral '36' mounted on the wheel of a Canada artillery cap badge, F J Coring, Sale 11, May 1998, Item 102; 72nd Battery CFA cap badge is the numerals '7' and '2' separately mounted on the wheel of a Canada artillery cap badge, Jeffrey Hoare, Sale 16, December 1994, Item 643.

7. Catalogue No 41-12-40. A gun over a scroll reading "40th Canadian F.A." It is catalogued as a collar badge. This badge was also in the Ray Salmon collection.

8. Cross, Corps, pp.203, 205-210, 212, 214-218, 220-234.

9. A/QMG to GOC MD No 2, 5 January 1918, 34-4-7 (Vol 5).

10. RG24, Vol 6497, 305-3-29 (Vol 4).

11. *Statement Regarding Badges of Canadian Units,* August 1916, *op cit.*

12. B-72-33

13. Cross Corps pp.236-237; Jeffrey Hoare Sale 52, February 1996, Item 3462, Sale 54, October 1996, Item 2737, Sale 55, February 1997, Item 2351.

14. Letter 23 February 1916, RG24, Vol 1564, 683-264-1.

15. In silver, the Canada artillery gun badge with 107 over a scroll reading Battery below the artillery motto, Guenter Requadt collection. No 3 Siege Battery was known as the 107th (Canadian) Siege Battery from February 1916 to January 1917.

16. RG9IIID.1, Vol 4685, Folder 33, File 8.

17. *ibid*, Folder 33, File 10.

18. Major-General Commanding 4th Canadian Division to Canadian Corps "Q", 27 August 1917, D-209-33.

Chapter 4: Line of Communication Units and Other Corps Badges
c1 to c27. These references are to the table of Cross' catalogue numbers at the end of the Chapter.

1. Colonel Commanding CTD to HQ CEF, 9 Nov 1916, 4-2-18; *Minute 3,* DOS to QMG, 13 June 1918, C-1013-33 (Vol 1).

2. Fort Garry Horse Museum and Archives.

3. MO 207/1917.

4. OC CLH to Camp Commandant, Canadian Corps, 2 August 1917, RG9IIIB.1, Vol 3298, C-23-43 (Vol 1).

5. Boulton James J, *Uniforms of the Canadian Mounted Police* (North Battleford 1990) pp.203-212; Glenbow Museum, Calgary, tunic and cap, Const. Harry C Douglass, B Squadron RNWMP, CEF (Siberia), Catalogue No C-51951A-B.

6. A sweetheart pin of collar badge size also exists similar to the badge in Figure 23.

7. Lieutenant-Colonel G S Canadians, Seaford to HQ Canadian Troops, Seaford, 8 August 1918, points out that "The Engineer Grenades should be "Canada" Grenades", C-1013-33. Only the plain grenade was ever made.

8. AG Canadian Militia to DOC MD 13, 3 August 1915, RG24, Vol 4726, 448-14-194

9. AG Canadian Militia to DOC MD 11, 15 August 1915, RG24, Vol 4763, 99-4-15-1.

10. RG9IIID.1, Vol 4709, Folder 92, Files 16, 17, 18.

11. *ibid*, Folder 92, File 18.

12. Adjutant for Labour Commandant to HQ Labour Group, 29 October 1918 refers to authority for special cap badges as Canadian Corps Q 28/56, 28 October 1918; OC Canadian Labour Group to The Goldsmiths and Silversmiths Company, 23 October 1918; RG9IIIC.6, Vol 4452, Folder 1, File 5.

13. RG9IIID.1, Vol 4709, Folder 93, Files 2, 4, 6, 8.

14. *Statement of Badges of Canadian Units,* August 1917, *op cit,* D-209-33; AD Signals Canadian Corps to Chief Engineer Canadian Corps, 6 March 1917, B-4-3; RG9IIID.l, Vol 4711, File 97, Folder 22, 4th Divisional Signals Company, Folder 25, 5th Divisional Signals Company.

15. *Statement of Badges of Canadian Units,* August 1917, *op cit.*

16. Quartermaster General to Chief of General Staff, 26 June 1916, RG24, Vol 1640, 593-16-1.

17. A/ADOS Canadian Corps to DOS, 2 September 1917, B-4-3.

18. Invoice H B Sale Limited, 12 July 1916 for badges, Ron Edward's research files.

19. Badges were ordered 28 December 1915, Coeur de Leon MacCarthy to OC Borden's Machine Gun Battery, Ron Edwards' research files.

20. Jacoby Bros quoted on the cap and collar badges, letter 18 February 1915, Ron Edward's research files.

21. Captain Commanding Eaton Motor Machine Gun Battery to Canadian War Records Office, 27 August 1917, RG9IIID.1, Vol 4687, Folder 38, File 10.

22. Lieutenant-Colonel R. Brutinel, Corps Machine Gun Officer asked permission for the units of the Motor Machine Gun Branch CMGC to wear a special emblem on the right upper sleeve of the Service Dress jacket, 21 May 1917, B-4-3. It is possible this was one of those special emblems.

23. The badge illustrated in Cross Corps p. 92 as a cap badge is a collar badge. The cap badge is larger. Capt H F Meurling to Canadian War Records Office, 3 July 1917 stated that the men were wearing the cap badge of Boyle's Yukon Machine Gun Detachment. Also the Battery Historical Record of the same date states "for present battery no special badges have been authorized, wherefore the men are carrying all kinds". (RG9IIID.1, Vol 4687, Folders 38 & 39)

24. OC Borden Motor Machine Gun Battery to Canadian War Records Office, 27 June 1917, RG9IIID.l, Vol 4687, Folder 38, File 7.

25. Replies to Canadian Corps "Q" to requests for information on badges in use, *op cit.* Badges claimed to be for some of the other machine gun companies (other than the 3rd, 4th, and 9th Companies) have appeared in auctions in the last few years. It is doubtful that these were used or at best were makeshift items.

26. *Statement Regarding Badges of Canadian Units,* August 1916, *op cit; Estimate of Badges required by 2nd Canadian Division,* 15 February 1917, shows these as requirements for its machine gun companies; *Summary of Badges required for the 4th Canadian Division,* 13 March 1917, shows these as requirements for its machine gun companies and Yukon Motor Machine Gun Battery; B-4-3.

27. B-4-3.

28. Brig-General R. Brutinel to Canadian Corps "Q", 5 December 1918, B-4-3 (Vol 2); Director of Equipment and Ordnance Stores, War Office to Secretary OMFC, 3 March 1919, C-1013-33 (Vol 2).

29. ADOS Canadian Corps to QMG OMFC, 14 December 1918, RG9IIIC.1, Vol 3926, Folder 2 File 8; QMG to J W Tiptaft & Son, 22 December 1918, C-1013-33 (Vol 2).

30. Commandant Canadian Machine Gun Depot to Canadian War Records Office, 26 December 1916, RG9IIID.1, Vol 4687, Folder 39, File 8.

31. A sterling silver crossed machine gun surmounted by a crown with Canada scroll below (device different from any collar badge seen) mounted on a plain bronze maple leaf. The maple leaf is unmarked but likely was made by Tiptaft. Ron Edwards collection.

32. QMG to Commanding Canadian Corps, 19 September 1918, C-1013-33 (Vol 2). OC 1st Canadian Motor Machine Gun Brigade to DADOS, 17 September 1918 states that the British Machine Gun Corps collar badges were being worn at the time (source unknown).

33. Browning copper maple leaf with collar badge in silver mounted thereon. Jeffrey Hoare Sale 59, June 1998, Item 1589.

Chapter 5: More Badges for Line of Communication Units and Other Corps

c1 to c69. These references are to the table of Cross' catalogue numbers at the end of the Chapter.

1. Letters to Historical Section, Canadian War Records Office RG9IIID.1, Vol 4713: OC 4th Divisional Train, 23 May 1917, Folder 103, File 11; OC 3rd Divisional Train, 9 July 1917, Folder 103, File 8; OC 3rd Divisional Supply Column, 3 July 1917, Folder 103, File 22.

2. The Author has not been able to identify the unit wearing these badges. There were three units numbered "7" in the CASC. No 7 Company CASC was a militia unit organized 1 Dec 1903 located in Saint John, N B. There was two No 7 units in the CEF. One was No 7 Depot Unit of supply that was mobilized in Montreal and served in France with the 2nd Canadian Division, the other was No 7 CASC Service Company located in Saint John, N.B.

3. 96-11-70 (Vol 1).

4. QMG Canadian Militia to DCO MD No 1, 26 March 1917 refers to badges for the Canadian Medical Corps as the "authorized sealed pattern", RG24, Vol 4260, 47-4-3. This badge was approved for the permanent force and militia after the war by GO 17/1924.

5. Cross incorrectly describes this badge as that of the 2nd Field Ambulance which was mobilized at Toronto from Ontario units west of Kingston.

6. The collar badge, which is 3 cm wide and 1.5 cm high, contains elements of the Arms of Dalhousie University i.e., an Earl's coronet, a shield containing a bird and a unicorn's head couped at the neck (figure 79). These were taken from the Arms of the Earl of Dalhousie. Following is a partial description of the badge from a study with a magnifying glass of a photograph of a group of badges belonging to the collection :

   A shield bearing an eagle with wings and legs outstretched, to the left an Earl's coronet, to the right a unicorn's head couped at the neck. Above the shield is a scroll* sur-

   Figure 82 Elements from the Arms of Dalhousie University

   mounted by the numeral '7'. On the left, a scroll reading "Canadian" joins the ducal crown and the numeral; on the right a scroll* joins the unicorn's head and the numeral. At the base of the ducal crown is a scroll*; and a scroll* is at the base of the unicorn's head.

   * the wording of these scrolls cannot be determined.

7. The badge was the CAMC badge with the Rod of Aesculapius removed and the unit abbreviation brazed in its place. The Author inspected the specimen in the collection of the late Bill Moffat and it appeared genuine and the brazing was of jeweller's quality. In response to the request for badges from the Historical Section the unit was only able to send their distinctive shoulder title.

8. Same design as the badge of the 9th Canadian Mounted Rifles badge with horseshoe scroll reading "Field Ambulance" and lower scroll reading "Canada", sterling with red, white and blue enamel, Canadian War Museum Catalogue No 46-30-300.

9. *Dress Regulations for Chaplains Canadian Contingents,* issued by the Office of the Senior Chaplain, 28 December 1916, RG9IIIB.1, Vol 416, File D-30-1.

10. It is believed the maple leaf was added without authority to each blade of the cross about two years after approval. Research into Canadian Chaplain's Badges by David Love, Calgary.

11. The square-styled cross collar badge[c16] on a General Service maple leaf cap badge. Bob Russell collection; It was stated in a letter from the Assistant Director of Chaplain Services (RC), CEF to Director of Chaplain Services CEF in late 1916 that the Maltese Cross badge "is not popular in the service and individuals have taken to wearing designs of their own making..." Research by David Love.

12. Letter 31 May 1917, RG9IIID.1, Vol 4718, Folder 113, File 30.

13. C-1013-33 (Vol 1).
14. This badge is not mentioned in Cross. The Author examined the badge in the collection of the late Bill Moffat. It was a genuine die stamped badge. The cypher GRV surmounted by a crown. A scroll extending from the top of the cypher reads "Provost Marshall Staff MD 10 Canada". Between the bottom of the cypher and above the scroll were crossed pistols.
15. The 5th Divisional Cyclist Company was never approved in General Orders. This was an unofficial designation of a company from the Divisional Cyclist Depot, Toronto. This company embarked for the UK during January 1917 and was broken up for reinforcements, Ellis, WD and Beatty, JG, *Saga of The Cyclists in The Great War 1914-1918* (Toronto, November 1965) pp.45-51.
16. Nos 1 and 2 Companies CFC at the front were organized in France in 1915. The 224th Battalion badges were approved February 1916 and the battalion arrived in the UK in four parties during May/June 1916. Nos 1 and 2 Parties of the 224th Battalion served in the UK. There also were Nos 1 and 2 Forestry Companies raised in Ontario during 1917.
17. The 122nd Battalion had been converted to a composite infantry and forestry unit in February 1917, *London Advertiser*, 21 February 1917.
18. Device is collar badge size with two wire fasteners for attachment to a badge. This may have been a test stamping. Author's collection. Officers were appointed for the Draft in MOs 113, 114, 128/1917.
19. Silver plated collar badge on browning copper plain maple leaf marked Tiptaft, Jeffrey Hoare Sale 59, June 1998, Item 1570.
20. Design of the 256th Railway Construction Corps badge with 'RCD' in place of '256'.
21. No 3 Section Skilled Railway Employees were formed October 1917. Its establishment was approved 19 December 1917, RG24, Vol 4616, File 8. However, authorization was never published in General Orders.
22. Babin 21-7, 1st issue cap badge.
23. The design was approved to be used on the note paper of the Depot in Canada, 34-4-7 (Vol 5); The OC CRT Depot at Purfleet, England stated to the Canadian War Records Office, 17 November 1917 that they had no special badges, RG9IIIC.7, Vol 4468, Folder 1, File 7.
24. Bone, *Alberta Units*, p.57.
25. The badge maker is J R Gaunt London.
26. AG Canadians to Secretary Militia Council, 25 January 1918; Various letters, B-72-33; RG9IIIC.7, Vol 4468, Folder 1, File 7.
27. OC 12th Battalion CRT to CRT Depot, 14 January 1918, refers to "badges recently approved in process of manufacture", RG9IIIC.1, Vol 4468, Folder 1, File 7.
28. ADOS 4/1, 27 October 1917, B-4-3.
29. ADOS to ADOS Canadian Corps, 6 June 1918, C-1013-33 (Vol 1).
30. GOC Corps Canadian Railway Troops to GOC Canadian Section, GHQ 1st Echelon, RG9IIIC.7, Vol 4472, Folder 1, File 2.
31. C-1013-33 (Vol 2).
32. Babin 32-2
33. A tank mounted on a General Service maple leaf. The tank is seen mounting either left or right. The shape of the maple leaf varies. Jeffrey Hoare Sale 58, February 1998, Item 2649 and Sale 59, June 1998, Item 1646.

Chapter 6: Badges of Other Services, Units and Organizations

b1 to b4, c1 to c25. These references are to the table of Babin's and Cross' catalogue numbers at the end of the Chapter.

1. Director of Clothing and Equipment to Director of Veterinary Services, 21 February 1916, RG9IIIB.1, Vol 3364, B-4-45.

2. Chief Paymaster to Canadian War Records Office, 28 May 1917, RG9IIID.1, Vol 4719, Folder 114, File 13.

3. QMG to Paymaster General OMFC, 17 September 1918, RG9IIIB.1, Vol 2765, D-157-33.

4. *Statement Regarding Badges of Canadian Units*, August 1916, *op cit.*

5. Officer i/c Postal Services OMFC to Canadian War Records Office, 16 May 1917, RG9IIID.1, Vol 4719, Folder 115, File 22.

6. J W Tiptaft & Son to Director of Ordnance Services, 16 December 1918, C-1013-33 (Vol 2).

7. *Regimental Badges Inventory of Badges on File*, 3 October 1917, RG9IIID.1, Vol 4720, Folder 118A, File 24; *Badges worn by Units of the Canadian Expeditionary Force*, compiled 1928 by the Historical Section (General Staff) on transfer of the collection to the Public Archives of Canada, RG24, Vol 1736, DHS 3-11 (Vol 3).

8. Stewart, Plate No 31, from Canadian War Museum collection.

9. *Monthly Reports Branches of the OMFC*, RG9IIIA.1, Vol 53.

10. In silver a beaver surmounted by a crown on a rectangular tablet reading "Canada" with a scroll below reading "General Headquarters", mounted on a browning copper maple leaf marked Hicks & Sons, London. Jeffrey Hoare Sale 59, June 1998, Item 1649.

11. These badges do not appear in *Regimental Badges Inventory of Badges on File, op cit*, or *Badges worn by Units of the Canadian Expeditionary Force, op cit*, However, the badges of the Corps of Guides was in the Will R Bird collections of CEF badges.

12. Badges of the Canadian School of Musketry did not appear on the Regimental *Badges Inventory of Badges on File*, but is in the Canadian War Museum collection, Stewart plate No 30.

13. This badge has a pin fastener. It is possible it was either worn on the sleeve or elsewhere on the work clothes. A specimen is included in the Will R Bird collection.

14. Chinese Labour personnel were recruited by the British Army for employment in France. They were formed into 195 "Chinese Labour Companies". They were transported from the Orient to France via Canada. Some were concentrated at a Camp in Petawawa awaiting transportation overseas. (*Chinese Coolies - Great War* , RG24, Vol 1833, GAQ 8-36.) It is possible that the item illustrated in Cross Corps 70-11-1 under the heading "Canadian Labour Company" was a tag for these Chinese workers. There is no reference in the CEF records to a unit known as the "Canadian Labour Company".

15. Jeffrey Hoare, Sale 7, September 1992, Item 477.

16. OC No 2 Special Service Companies, 21 February 1918, 34-4-7 (Vol 5)

17. Jeffrey Hoare, Sale 57, October 1997, Item 2276. The numeral "6" is in silver brazed over the numeral of a No 2 Special Service Company badge. The badge is marked "Rosenthal".

18. The badge is marked "J R Gaunt London" and has lugs.

19. A specimen of this badge in the Author's collection has its original lugs.

20. Bone, *British Columbia Units*, p. 63.

21. *The Toronto Daily News,* 28 October 1916.

22. The first parade of the Portage la Prairie Home Guard was held on 31 August, 1914, *Manitoba Free Press*, 1 September 1914; for the Toronto Home Guard, 2 October 1914, *The Toronto Daily News,* 3 October 1914; for the Hamilton Home Guard, 29 October 1914, *Toronto World,* 30 October 1914; for the Montreal Home Guard, 18 November 1914, *The Gazette, Montreal,* 19 November 1914

23. Members of the Toronto Home Guard formed the nucleus of the 109th Regiment (authorized 15 December 1914) in the militia. Later the Toronto Home Guard became the reserve battalion of the 109th Regiment. *The Toronto Daily News,* 5 January and 26 May 1915.

24. Canadian War Museum collection.

25. Later became part of the Reserve Militia as the 1st Regiment Reserve Militia, Montreal Home Guard, GO 18, 1 March 1916.

26. Formed during July 1916, *The Morning Bulletin,* Edmonton, 10 July 1916.

27. Originally formed as a Home Guard unit on 1 October 1915, *Manitoba Free Press,* 1 October 1915. Later became part of the Reserve Militia, GO 18, 1 March 1916.

28. Authorized GO 53, 1 June 1916.

29. Marway Militaria, Sale 43, March 1997, Item S348: within a voided oval the letter Q over HG, cast badge painted black.

30. The Edmonton Reserve Militia Battalion was formed June 1916 with personnel of the Legion of Frontiersmen Infantry Battalion automatically becoming members. *The Morning Bulletin,* Edmonton, 30 June 1916. It held its first parade on 28 June 1916, *The Edmonton Journal,* 29 June 1916.

31. *The Morning Bulletin,* Edmonton, 1 July 1916. The lapel pin was likely the logo of the Legion of Frontiersmen, as this logo was part of the heading on Battalion Orders (see inset) published in the newspapers .

32. Their first drill was held 31 July 1916, *The Edmonton Journal,* 31 July 1916.

33. Tyler, Grant, *The Winnipeg Women's Volunteer Reserve,* Journal of the Military History Society of Manitoba 1997, pp.19-21

Chapter 7: Shoulder Titles

c1 to c26. These references are to the table of Cross' catalogue numbers at the end of the Chapter.

1. Hicks & Sons to Canadian War Records Office, 10 April 1916, RG9IIID.1, Vol 4720, Folder 118A, File 15; OC 160th Battalion to AAG MD No 1, 10 May 1916, RG24, Vol 4260, 47-3-13.

   Descriptions of cloth shoulder titles are as follows:

1st Battalion	CANADA over 1, blue on khaki
3rd Battalion	TORONTO, blue on khaki
5th Battalion	WESTERN CAVALRY over 5th, yellow on khaki
6th Battalion	FORT GARRY'S over 6th, yellow on black
7th Battalion	BRITISH COLUMBIA, green on khaki
8th Battalion	90th RIFLES, green on khaki
9th Battalion	EDMONTON over 101st over 9, red on khaki
12th Battalion	CANADA over 12, red on khaki

   Jeffrey Hoare, Sale 55, February 1997, Item 2520, Sale 12, April 1994, Item 969; Photograph Cpl 7th Battalion CEF; OC 2nd Infantry Brigade to AAG i/c Administration, RG9IIIC.3, Vol 4045, Folder 2, File 3; Royal Winnipeg Rifles Regimental Museum, Glenbow Museum; Author's collection: Hemsleys (Montreal) *Revised List of Woven Titles & Embroidered Badges etc,* RG9IIID.1, Vol 4720, Folder 118A, File 12.

2. Cited in QMG to CGS, 1 May 1915, RG24 Vol 1485, 683-1-4.

3. MO 164, 29 March 1915 *Canadian Expeditionary Force - Clothing and Equipment of.* This cancelled and replaced MO 524, 23 November 1914 as amended by MO 11, 4 January 1915; QMG Canadian Militia to OC Divisions and Military Districts, 12 January 1915, RG24, Vol 1507, 683-2-1.

4. Carson to COO, 21 April 1915, 4-2-18.

5. Circular letter to all DOC's, GOC's and Camp Commandants, Valcartier and Petawawa, RG24, Vol 6497, 305-3-29 (Vol 2).

6. COO CEF to Secretary War Office, 25 May 1916, B-4-3.

7. B-4-3.

8. It appears that in practice the shoulder title CGA was worn by Siege Artillery Batteries instead of the shoulder title SA referred to in the Dress Regulations.
9. RG9IIIB.1, Vol 2766, D-172-33.
10. ADOS 4/1, 27 October 1917, B-4-3.
11. COO to Carson, 17 February 1916, 4-2-18.
12. These cloth shoulder titles are known for infantry battalions (other than those of the 1st Contingent) and depot battalions:

PPCLI	P.P.C.L.I., white on red*
27th Battalion	27 over CITY OF WINNIPEG, blue on khaki
31st Battalion	31st ALBERTA, white on khaki
46th Battalion	46 CANADA, green letters and border on red
49th Battalion	49 over CANADA, red on khaki
105th Battalion	PRINCE EDWARD ISLAND, blue on khaki
160th Battalion	160 over BRUCE, white on red
166th Battalion	unknown lettering on khaki*
198th Battalion	198 over CANADA, gold bullion wire on khaki
207th Battalion	CANADA over 207, red on black*
217th Battalions	details unknown*
244th Battalion	KITCHENER'S OWN over CANADA, gold on khaki
255th Battalion	Q.O.R. over 255 over CANADA, red on khaki*
unknown	CALGARY, blue on khaki
unknown	ONTARIO, blue on khaki
1st Depot Bn Alberta Regt	ALBERTA, blue on khaki

    *Approved - see Appendix 4

    Hemsleys (Montreal) *Revised List of Woven Titles & Embroidered Badges etc, op. cit*; *A History of the 160th Overseas Bruce Battalion,* Walkerton, Ont 1934, Section on badges; Marway Militaria, Sale 33, 1995; Prince Edward Island Regiment Military Museum, Wyn van der Schee collection, Tom Gudmestad collection; Uniform of Milton S McDougall, 1st Depot Battalion, Alberta Regiment, Glenbow Museum Catalogue C17390; Notes compiled by Bill Alexander, North Bay, Ont.
13. Uniform of Cpl Mascaro, 25th Battalion, Glenbow Museum No C9586; Uniform of Pte Harry Ritz, 78th Battalion, Glenbow Museum, No WS-190; Uniform of Sgt E M Peacock, 102nd Battalion, Provincial Museum of Alberta, Accession 868.81.1. In each case, the C over numeral collar badge was on the shoulder straps above the CANADA title, and the battalion pattern collar badges were on the uniform.
14. GOC, SSO MD No 2 to DAA & QMG MD No 2, 27 October 1917, 34-4-47 (Vol 5).
15. Jeffrey Hoare, Sale 50, June 1995, Item 2451.
16. Prince Edward Island Regiment Military Museum.
17. OC 11th Canadian Siege Battery to Canadian War Records Office, 7 February 1918, RG9IIID.1, Vol 4685, Folder 33, File 10.
18. Included in the Inventory *Badges worn by Units of the Canadian Expeditionary Force, op cit.*
19. Glenbow Archives Photograph NA-5035-15, LCpl Gerald Fuller, 12th Regiment Canadian Mounted Rifles.
20. Glenbow Archives Photograph NA-4755-1, Pte C H Woollven, 13th Regiment Canadian Mounted Rifles.
21. HQ 4th Division, *Minute No 11,* 15 June 1916, 4-2-18.
22. *Dress Regulations for Canadian Units, op cit.*
23. This title was submitted to the Canadian War Records Office in 1917 by No 1 Tunnelling

Company, RG9IIID.1, Vol 4711, Folder 96, File 11. The title T.C was also approved for the Canadian Tank Corps April 1918.

24. Tom Gudmestad collection. The 107th Pioneer Battalion from Winnipeg was absorbed by the 1st, 2nd, 3rd Battalions Canadian Engineers in May 1918. These battalions were demobilized in Winnipeg on 7 May 1919.

25. *Statement Regarding Badges of Canadian Units*, August 1916, *op cit*.

26. Wore the same shoulder title as the Yukon Infantry Company illustrated in Cross Infantry p.262, Canadian War Museum collection Catalogue No 41-29-5-4-1. A photograph of an officer in the Yukon Motor Machine Gun Battery shows him wearing this title, Tim Popp collection.

27. Titles submitted to the Historical Section, Canadian War Records Office, Summer 1917 by OC Canadian Machine Gun Depot, RG9IIID.1, Vol 4687, Folder 39, File 8.

28. Photographs show that this title often being worn with CMGC badges illustrated in Cross 45-1-9.

29. Title submitted 15 May 1917 by OC 3rd Machine Gun Company, RG9IIID.1, Vol 4686, Folder 36, File 16. Title is now in the Canadian War Museum collection.

30. Uniform of a member of Eaton Motor Machine Gun Battery, Victor Taboika Elbow War Museum collection, Calgary; Canadian War Museum collection.

31. Military Secretary to The Chief of the General Staff, RG24, Vol 1485, 683-1-4.

32. Glenbow Museum collection.

33. Jeffrey Hoare Sale 59, June 1998, Item 1583.

34. DAG Orgn to DEOS, 5 July 1918 and DEOS to DAG Org, 24 February 1919, RG24, Vol 1201, 96-11-97.

35. Worn by C.Q.M.Sgt. W Floyd Shaw of Vegreville, Alberta, Author's collection. The Syren Party left Scotland for Russia on 18 September 1918, RG24, Vol 1742, DHS 4-21.

Chapter 8: Odds and Ends

c1 to c13. These references are to the table of Cross' catalogue numbers at the end of the Chapter.

1. Brooker Chris, *The Standard Catalogue of Canadian Army Badges 1885 to date, Book 2*, p.15.

2. Durand collection; Babin 40-2.

3. This is the badge of the Clan Campbell of Breadalbane with the centre removed and a Canadian die collar badge with the wolfe's head sinister mounted on the belted circlet.

4. Durand collection and *Notes on Pipe Band Badges* compiled by the late Leslie Whitford, Toronto, July 1957. He carried out extensive research on the dress and insignia of CEF highland units and pipe bands. The picture of the 224th Battalion pipe band badge in Cross (30-1-2) is not the genuine badge. While it closely resembles the genuine badge, it is a 96th Battalion cap badge (Cross 96) with the centre of the Canadian Forestry Corps cap badge (30-1-1A) placed in the centre. The collector who created this badge showed it to the Author before he had it silver plated.

5. Ian Edwards of Sherwood Park, Alberta has done extensive research on the insignia of the 49th Battalion Pipe Band. The 49th Battalion badge incorporating the windmill was approved and introduced between August and October 1916. However all the members of the 49th Battalion Pipe Band but one had been loaned to the PPCLI during March and April 1916 where they remained until the end of the war. Pictures of the Pipe Band of The Edmonton Regiment during 1920-24 shows this badge worn by that band. He will be publishing an article on his research in the Journal of The Military Collectors' Club of Canada.

6. Whitford, *Notes on Pipe Band Badges*.

7. The late Capt J J Claxton, Irish Fusiliers of Canada badge collector and curator of the Regimental Museum wrote this to the Author in the 1960s. This was told to him by Pipe

Major McCullough who took the pipe band to France. McCullough's badge was in the Regimental Museum in the Armoury which was completely destroyed by fire. Reference to the presentation of the banner appears in Clyne, H R N, *Vancouver's 29th* (Vancouver 1964) p.152, but no mention is made of the presentation of the Clan badges.

8. Durand collection re 224th Bn; Stewart p.97, 99, 102.
9. Saskatoon Public Library, Photograph LH6294, Pipe Band 96th Overseas Battalion Canadian Highlanders, Camp Hughes 1916.
10. Stewart p.15.
11. *ibid* p.78, 99.
12. Uniform of a member of the 13th Battalion, Victor Taboika Elbow War Museum collection, Calgary.
13. Uniform of John Sheard, 15th Battalion, Victor Taboika Elbow War Museum collection, Calgary; Information from 48th Highlanders Museum, Toronto.
14. Stewart p. 9; Uniform of a member of the 16th Battalion, Victor Taboika Elbow War Museum collection, Calgary.
15. Information from Queen's Own Cameron Highlanders of Canada Museum, Winnipeg; Picture of 179th Battalion at Minto Barracks, April 1916, Victor Taboika Elbow War Museum collection, Calgary.
16. Uniform of a member of the 72nd Battalion, Victor Taboika Elbow War Museum collection, Calgary; Information from Seaforth Highlanders off Canada Regimental Museum.
17. Uniform of Edward Hughes, MM, 85th Battalion, Victor Taboika Elbow War Museum collection, Calgary; *85th Canadian Infantry Battalion Dress Regulations*, RG9IIID.1, Vol 4698, Folder 65, File 16; Information from The Army Museum, Halifax Citadel.
18. Information from 48th Highlanders Museum, Toronto.
19. Pictures of soldiers of the 173rd Battalion Charles Hamilton collection (One is found in Law, Clive M, *Khaki: Uniforms of the Canadian Expeditionary Force* p.27); Wyn van der Schee, Calgary, collection; Ontario Archives, Toronto.
20. Historical Record 42nd Battalion, RG9IIID.1, Vol 4695, Folder 57, File 14; Stewart p.37, re 73rd Battalion.
21. These badges all have devices (indicated in 'quotes') mounted on the General Service maple leaf:

3rd Battalion	'collar badge' (Jeffrey Hoare, Sale 55, February 1997, Item 2370)
	'3' (*Ibid*, Item 2371)
7th Battalion	'7' (*Ibid*, Item 2372)
9th Battalion	'C over 9' (Marway, Sale 18, August 1992, Item C202)

22. The 20th badge has the letters and numerals brazed on a General Service maple leaf marked "P W Ellis Co 1914". The 157th badge has numerals brazed on an unmarked General Service maple leaf. The 177th badge has the numerals in white letters brazed on a General Service maple leaf marked "Geo H Lees & Co 1915".
23. These badges are as follows:

    3rd Battalion (Cross 3A)

    7th Battalion (Cross 7B)

    19th, 122, 157th, 177th Battalions (Cross 19D, 122C, 157B, 177B)

    > these were made by Caron Bros and are exactly the same design as the approved badge worn by the 91st Battalion

    104th, 110th, 118th and 118th Battalions (Cross 104B, 110B, Jeffrey Hoare, Sale)

    16, December 1994, Item 550 and Cross 118B)

    > these were made by Caron Bros and are exactly the same design as the unapproved badge worn by the 71st Battalion. The 110th and 115th had pin fasteners, so they may have been brooches.

63rd, 66th, 138th and 151st Battalion (Cross 63B, 66B, 138B, 151D) these were all recruited in Edmonton and area. The Author has seen only collar size badges of this design. The 63rd badge has original lugs; the other three have pin fasteners and are obviously sweetheart pins.

24. Glenbow Museum, Calgary, Catalogue No C-9317: silver plated collar badge riveted on a bronze maple leaf. There is no maker's name, but the maple leaf is of the Tiptaft type. It appears genuine.

25. Both badges are the unit collar badge in silver mounted on a plain maple leaf, Jeffrey Hoare Sale 59, June 1998, Items 1570 and 1589.

26. Sgt Thomas Bradley, a cousin of the Author's wife, served in the 147th during its existence and later with the 4th Canadian Mounted Rifles Battalion in France until the armistice. After the war he was an active member of the 147th Battalion Association. He lived in Milton, Ont and died at age 94.

27. The 147th Battalion badge is from the Author's collection, the others are from the Bob Russell collection. The 88th Battalion badge is marked "Tiptaft". The 101st Battalion badge is the design of the 106th Regiment "Winnipeg Light Infantry" with the numeral 101 brazed therein.

28. Cross Corps pp.236-237.

29. Jeffrey Hoare, Sale 52, February 1996, Item 3462; Sale 54, October 1996, Item 2737; Sale 55, February 1997, Item 2351.

30. HQ OMFC Argyll House, Summary of letter written 24 October 1917 for specimens of badges and replies received during October to December 1917, B-72-33.

31. Told to the Author by the late Bill Stewart, Curator, The Royal Canadian Military Institute and badge collector.

Epilogue

a1 to a21, c1 to c30. These references are to the table of Mazeas' and Cross' catalogue numbers at the end of the Chapter.

1. Militia Headquarters circular letters 226 and 231, 1921 incorporated in MO 297, 10 June 1925.

2. For example the CO of The Toronto Regiment wrote to HQ MD No 2, 28 February 1929:
   . . . Further, may it be pointed out that we are not, in the conventional sense "perpetuating" the Third Battalion. We are the Third Battalion. The Officer Commanding, the Second in Command, the Adjutant, the Signalling Officer, the Quartermaster and the Chaplain; all Company Commanders, two Company Seconds-in command; the R.S.M., R.Q.M's, all C.S.M's and C.Q.M.S's, about half the Sergeants, and some of the rank and file, actually served with the Third Battalion. (DHH, 325.009(D221), MD2 21-1-23)

3. Bone *British Columbia Units,* p.11.

4. There are two types of this badge. The CEF type is illustrated in Cross 14. A later type, in yellow brass and made by Scully for the militia regiment, has the points of the maple leaf intersecting the words in the garter motto at different places.

5. There are two versions of this badge. The CEF version has three separate numerals III (Babin E-3) and was made by Rosenthal, Toronto and Tiptaft, Birmingham. This version appears in the Canadian War Museum, Durand, Will Bird and Valour Road Legion collections of CEF badges. Another version has the numerals III joined together at the top and bottom (Cross 3B). This one was made by J R Gaunt and is illustrated in their post-war catalogue. It would appear this latter version was made for The Toronto Regiment of the militia.

6. Bone *British Columbia Units,* p. 41.

7. Based on a photograph of the unit on parade seen by Bill Elms.

8. A new cap badge (Mazeas M.18a) was approved for the regiment by GO1, 1924. The CO The Toronto Regiment wrote MD No 2, 9 November [year not stated]:

   . . . the last lot of cap badges supplied to us were so badly made that they have never been issued. The entire shipment is still unused. (DHH op.cit.)

   These badges were never issued to the Regiment.

9. The late Capt J J Claxton acted as Quartermaster at summer camps in the 1930s and recalled seeing some members of The Kootenay Regiment wearing 54th Battalion badges.

Bibliography

Primary Documents

Record Group 9III of the National Archives of Canada, *Records of The Overseas Military Forces of Canada and The Canadian Expeditionary Force, 1914-1922:* Frequently referenced files:

> 4-2-18 Minister of Overseas Military Forces of Canada: *Regimental Badges.* General Correspondence on policy and approvals of badges; correspondence with suppliers (Vol 8)
>
> B-4-3 (3 Vols) Canadian Corps Headquarters in France: *Approval and ordering of badges* (Vol 884)
>
> B-72-33 Argyll House, London (Headquarters of the Overseas Military Forces of Canada): *Badges Regimental* (Vol 2688)
>
> C-1013-33 Argyll House, London: *Supplies of Badges.* Mainly correspondence with J W Tiptaft & Son Ltd, Birmingham (Vol 2744)
>
> D-209-33 Argyll House, London: *Designations Units.* Includes information on badges (Vol 2771)
>
> C-23-43 (2 Vols) Quartermaster General, London: *Badges and general questions on Dress.* Includes correspondence with suppliers re ordering of badges; correspondence re policy on and authorization of badges (Vol 3298)

Record Group 24 of the National Archives of Canada, *Records of The Department of National Defence* contains files of individual units regarding badges. Frequently referenced files:

> 34-4-7 (5 Vols) Military District No 2: *Approval of Badges* (Vols 4347-4348)
>
> 96-11-70 (3 Vols) *Designation and Badges* (Vol 6403)

National Defence Headquarters, *Records of the Director of History and Heritage:* contains files on badges after World War I.

Published Works

Army Historical Section: *The Regiments and Corps of The Canadian Army,* Ottawa, 1964

Babin, Lenard L: *Cap Badges of The Canadian Expeditionary Forces 1914-1919 Illustrated,* Rochester, NY, not dated

Canada and The Great War, 6 Volumes, Toronto, 1917-21

Cross, W K, *The Charlton Standard Catalogue of First World War Canadian Infantry Badges,* 2nd Edition, Toronto, 1994

Cross, W K, *The Charlton Standard Catalogue of First World War Canadian Corps Badges,* Toronto, 1995

Duguid, Colonel A Fortescue: *Official History of The Canadian Forces in The Great War*

1914-1919. Volume 1, 1 August 1914 - September 1915, and Appendix, Ottawa, 1938

Law, Clive M.: *Khaki — Uniforms of the Canadian Expeditionary Force*, Ottawa, 1998

Mazeas, Daniel: *Canadian Militia Badges Pre 1914*, Saint-Brieuc, France, 1990

Mazeas, Daniel: *Canadian Badges 1920-1950,* Revised Edition, Saint-Brieuc, France, 1985

Nicholson, Colonel G W L: *Canadian Expeditionary Force 1914-1919*, Ottawa, 1962 *Report of The Ministry Overseas Military Forces of Canada 1918*, London, England

Stewart, Charles H: *"Overseas": The Lineages and Insignia of The Canadian Expeditionary Force 1914-1919*, Toronto, 1970

Badge Collections and Notes

Bird, Will R: *Photographs of CEF Badge Collection*. Bird was a Nova Scotia author and lived in Halifax, NS. He served in the 42nd Battalion, started collecting in the trenches and collected until the late 1940s.

Bone, Will R: *Notes on British Columbia Units; Notes on Alberta Units; Notes on Saskatchewan Units; Notes on Manitoba Units; More Notes on Western Canadian Military Badges*. Bone was Captain in The British Columbia Regiment (Duke of Connaught's Own Rifles).

Clawson, Major W K: *Notes on Badges 1st to 60th Battalions*. Clawson lived in Saint John, NB, served in the CEF from 1915. He was commissioned in The Saint John Fusiliers after the war and collected until the late 1940s.

Canadian War Museum: *Collection of CEF Badges,* originally assembled by the Historical Section Canadian War Records Office during 1917-18.

Duncan, Robert S: *Notes on CEF Badges,* Duncan lived in Toronto. He collected from after the war until the 1940s.

Durand, Captain Philippe: *Photographs of CEF Badge Collection*. Durand was Curator, People's Palace Museum, Glasgow, Scotland. He started collecting during the war.

Hill-Tout, Charles B: *Photographs from CEF Badge Collection,* These were included in Bone's Notes above. Hill-Tout served in the Canadian Forestry Corps CEF and collected until the 1950s.

Russell, Bob: *Collection of CEF Badges,* Russell currently collects and lives in Victoria, BC.

Valour Road Branch, Royal Canadian Legion, Winnipeg, *Photographs of Memorial CEF Badge Collection*. The collection was assembled by Dick Cox, Winnipeg.